Introduction

This collection of 101 appliqué block designs has been selected or designed for the beginning to intermediate quilt maker. Many of the designs can be combined into more complex forms by quilters with more experience.

The patterns are designed to fit comfortably on a 9½" square of background fabric. There are general instructions for using a photocopy machine to enlarge or reduce the images for use on larger or smaller blocks.

An appliqué design is made of fabric shapes applied to a background fabric using a stitching or fusing method. Appliqué designs are most often used to express the curving lines of nature, tools, and other things not particularly suited to the geometric patterns of ordinary patchwork.

One of the joys of appliqué is being able to select and use fabrics that you might never use in a patchwork quilt. You will find yourself on a quest for unusual textures and color combinations–just to create that special flower or leaf–and you won't need to buy vast quantities of yardage to create your dream. You'll join the ranks of those buying four yards of fabric–in one-eighth yard increments!

Hand or sewing machine techniques complete the designs. Basic instructions for hand and machine work are included. For more complete instructions, I suggest reading a copy of my book, ***Learn to do Appliqué in Just One Weekend*** (ASN #4179).

The designs in this collection are images of universal appeal for decorative arts. They are simple images that share the symbolism of fine appliqué and other art, but I've designed them following the sage advice, forgiving nature, and good humor of my students.

I hope your adventure in using these designs will be fun-filled and produce lively quilts. ❧

General Directions

How to Use These Designs

The blocks in this collection all fit within an 8" square, but the background fabric should be cut no smaller than 9½" square. General instructions for enlarging or reducing the patterns are included below.

The patterns do not include a seam allowance. Each part of the design will require a ¼" seam allowance to be added when cutting out the shapes from fabric.

Stitches used to apply the appliqué pieces should be firm and close together, no more than ⅛" apart.

When choosing blocks for your quilt, don't feel limited to those that are shown with the same background fabric, for example, blocks #63, 64 and 65. While these blocks look lovely together, you do not have to use just those blocks in a quilt. Pick your favorite blocks and use fabrics that tie the blocks together.

There are also blocks that may not seem to go with any others based on the background fabric. For example, Block #2, Dragonfly's Delight, has a light blue fabric background not used anywhere else. If you choose a background similar to that used in Block #6 or Block #95, it would fit perfectly.

Use your imagination and fabric stash to come up with your own perfect combination of blocks.

How to Reduce or Enlarge the Designs

Most communities offer an abundance of self-serve photocopy or duplicating service shops. The percentages suggested are those I have found useful and available on local machines. Because you will be working within the limits of your available copy machines you may need to experiment with the percentages.

The suggested percentages below will give you a comfortable margin of background fabric around the design. Some of us like to crowd the design right up to the seam allowance and some of us like to float the design on a bigger background. Test the sizes and designs before committing to a large project.

Reductions:

75% of original = 6" block
50% of original = 4" block

Enlargements:

125% of original = 10" block
150% of original = 12" block
175% of original = 14" block
200% of original = 16" block

Making and Using Templates

Create permanent appliqué templates for each pattern piece from thin cardboard. Trace outline of each pattern piece onto freezer paper. Iron freezer paper, shiny side down, to the cardboard. Cut patterns from cardboard with either a craft knife or scissors. Appliqué templates do not include the seam allowance.

Marking the Templates

Write the name of the pattern and mark any special instructions you might need on each pattern piece.

Especially make note of overlapping and under-lapping pieces, **Fig 1**.

Fig 1

Basic Supplies for Appliqué Quilts

Fabric

Select fabrics of 100% cotton. Cotton fabrics are stable and hold a fold when creased or pressed. Fabrics should not fray when cut with scissors. Other kinds of fabrics can be used by experienced quilters for special projects.

Color and Visual Texture

There is only one rule regarding the choice of color or visual texture: There should be enough contrast between the background and the applied fabrics to clearly communicate the design. The amount of contrast between the background and the applied fabrics is a matter of personal taste. Remember, however, that you want others to enjoy the designs you've chosen, so make sure there is enough contrast.

Supplies and Tools

Choose your tools carefully. To begin, buy good, sharp needles, matching threads, embroidery scissors, 100% cotton fabrics, and a good needle threader. You will discover for yourself any additional supplies and tools you need.

- **Hand Needles:** Use sharps–very fine, sharp, somewhat flexible, needles designed for hand stitching and appliqué.
- **Machine Needles:** Use a sharp needle with an eye large enough to accommodate the thread you use. A 70/10 needle was used for the machine sample blocks.
- **Appliqué Pins:** These pins are short, 1" to 1¼", thin and very sharp. They have small heads.
- **Bias Bars:** For making vines and stems. Metal bars in ⅛ inch, 3/16 inch and ¼ inch sizes were used for the photographed blocks.

- **Cardboard:** Poster-board or manila file folders are the correct weight for block and design templates.
- **Craft or Hobby Knife:** Very sharp, bladed knife for cutting cardboard or multiple layers of freezer paper.
- **Freezer Paper:** Coated paper used as a foundation for appliqué and for making cardboard templates. Find this product at the grocery store.
- **Fusible Webbing:** A paper-backed, [illegible]

[illegible] h or sizing for resizing fabrics after they have been pre-washed.

- **Stylus:** Sharp point for helping hold appliqué close to the machine needle or turning under the seam allowance close to the sewing machine.
- **Thimble:** Use a thimble for hand appliqué since both ends of the appliqué needle are sharp.
- **Thread:** Use a fine dressmaker's-weight thread (#60 or higher) that matches the piece being applied. If an exact match can't be found, use a slightly duller or darker color to blend into the shadows of the appliqué. For decorative machine stitching, use #50 or lower.
- **Hand Embroidery Thread:** A soft, decorative, six-ply thread used for embellishment. Do not use embroidery thread (also called embroidery floss) to apply the fabric to the background.
- **Monofilament Nylon Thread:** These very fine threads are strong and wear well. They come in clear and smoky gray colors that blend well with both the appliqué and background fabrics.
- **Machine Embroidery Thread:** Firm, decorative, threads in a variety of fiber content and weight. Excellent for embellishment.
- **Wooden Toothpicks:** For help in tucking under pesky seam allowances.

Nice-to-Have

- **Light Table or Box:** For transferring the designs from paper to the background fabric.

  As a good substitute, tape design and fabric to a window to transfer the design; or use a heavy, clear plastic sheet resting between two tables with a lamp placed below.

Appliqué Stitches

Hand Stitching

There are advantages to hand appliqué. It can be relaxing, fun, and it's portable.

Invisible Stitch

The Invisible Stitch is the stitch most commonly preferred by quilters making heirloom quality hand appliqué quilts and it takes a little practice to perfect. It is a hidden stitch made at 1/8"-maximum intervals through the side fold of the seam allowance. Push needle through seam allowance fold from backside; then, pull needle completely through fold. Note that needle is almost horizontal to the background fabric when the thread is pulled through the fold.

Next, place needle slightly under fold, push through background fabric and back through seam allowance fold, **Fig 2**. A little tug after each stitch secures the thread.

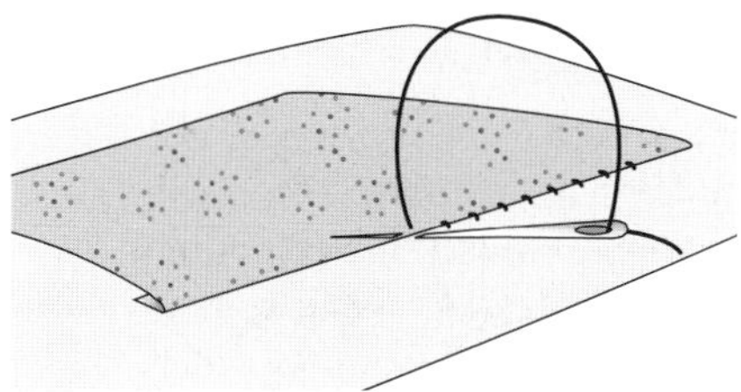

Fig 2

Blanket Stitch

The Blanket Stitch, **Fig 3**, gives a nice finished edge to appliqué, especially unturned edges.

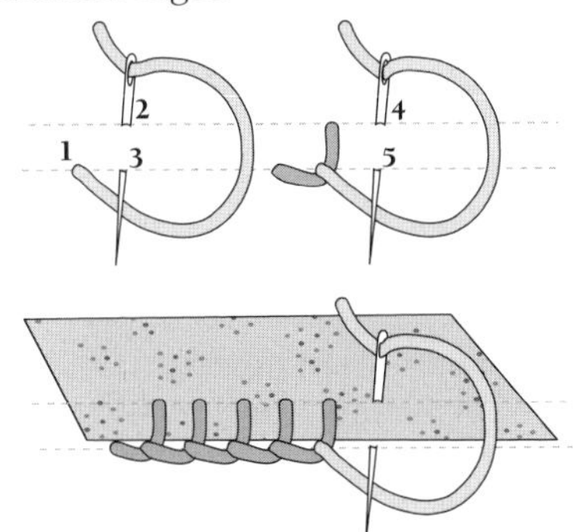

Fig 3

Machine Stitching

A significant influence on quilts today is the use of the sewing machine for appliqué. One would be wrong to think that sewing machines were commonly used for appliqué only with the arrival of the zigzag stitch machine. Many wonderful late nineteenth century quilts have the appliqué pieces topstitched by machine!

Machine appliqué is faster and stronger than hand appliqué and for many quilters it is a reasonable alternative to handwork.

Read your sewing machine manual to analyze the kinds of stitches your sewing machine can make. You will need to experiment with stitch style, thread tension, and length and width of stitch for the best possible results. A machine appliqué foot, with an open-under channel is used for most of these stitches. Thread type and color are critical in machine appliqué, particularly when thread tension is problematic. Keep a notepad handy to record particularly useful combinations of width and length.

Topstitch

Any sewing machine can topstitch appliqué pieces to the background fabric, **Fig 4**. It is a very strong stitch. Use with a turned-under seam allowance.

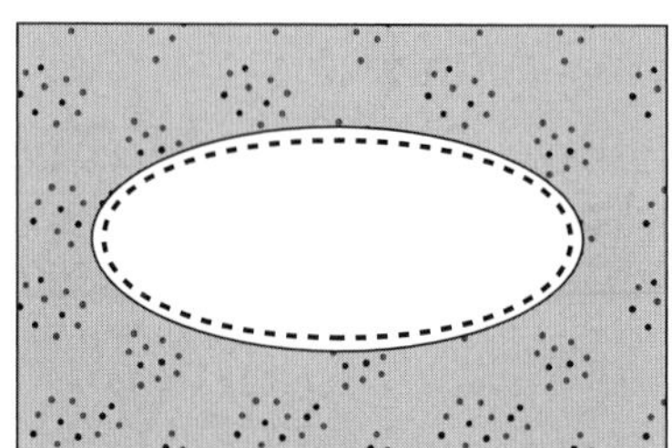

Fig 4

Blind Hem

The blind hem stitch, **Fig 5**, can almost duplicate the look of invisible hand appliqué.

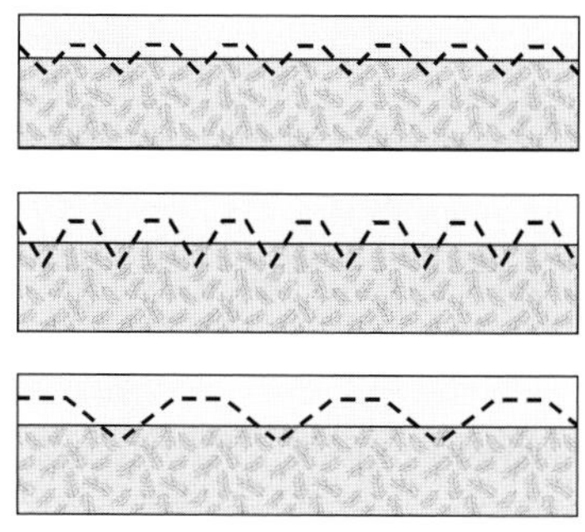

Fig 5

Thread color and the relationship between the appliqué edge and needle is critical. Experiment with stitch width, length and type of thread best suited for the results you want.

Zigzag Stitch

Use a zigzag stitch, **Fig 6**, with a short stitch length and width to almost duplicate the appearance of a whipped stitched edge. Thread color and the relationship between the appliqué edge and needle is critical.

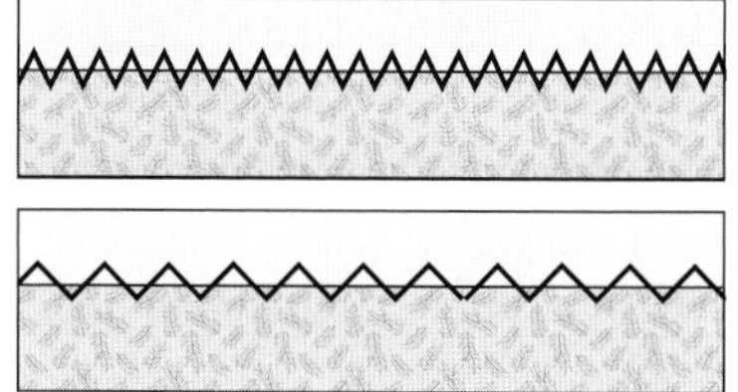

Fig 6

Blanket Stitch

A small, close machine blanket stitch, **Fig 7**, can almost duplicate a traditional hand stitch technique for finishing an unturned appliqué edge.

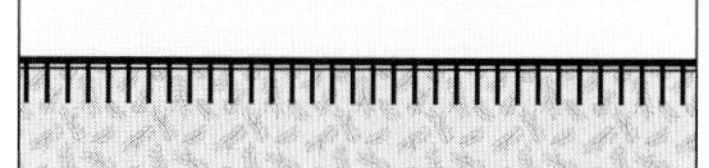

Fig 7

A larger machine blanket stitch gives the look of current folk-art-style appliqué and the appliqué from the 1920s and '30s, **Fig 8**.

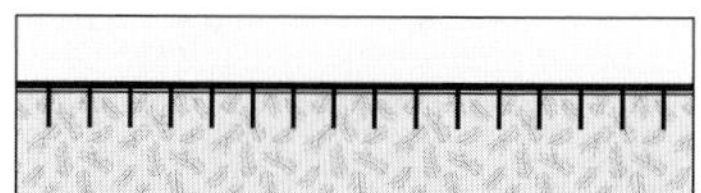

Fig 8

Satin Stitch

The satin stitch, **Fig 9**, is a heavy duty utility stitch for appliqué.

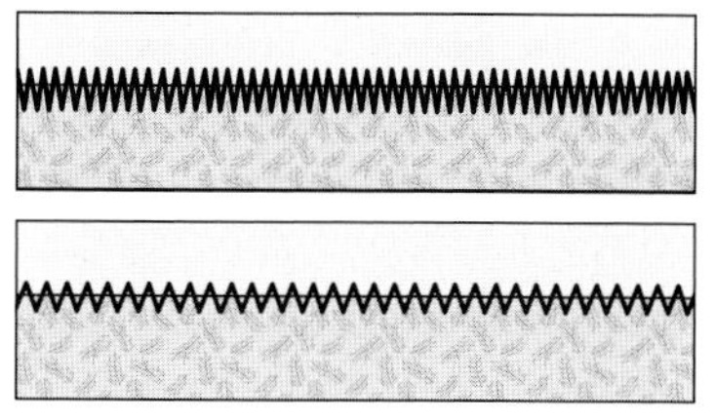

Fig 9

This stitch gives a strong decorative outline to the design. It is the slowest of the machine techniques.

Timely Tips:

Always stop your needle in the down, dropped, position when you machine appliqué.

When applying curved pieces you will drop the needle, pivot the fabric around the needle and stitch. Remember to: drop, pivot, stitch; drop, pivot, stitch; repeat.

Always SLOW DOWN AT CURVES!

Appliqué Design Extras

Window Templates

Window templates, **Fig 10**, allow you to take the best advantage of your fabric.

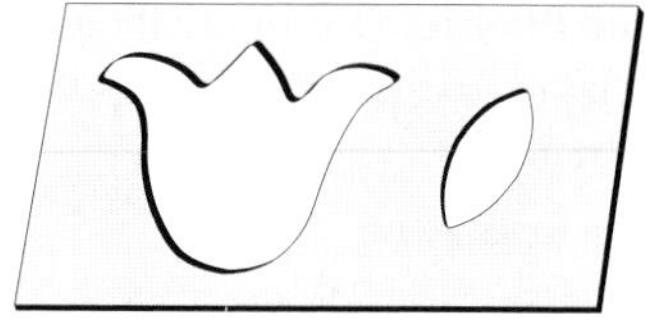

Fig 10

Trace appliqué designs onto a piece of cardboard. Leave an inch or two between each shape. Cut the silhouettes out with a craft knife. Clearly label the right side of the template sheet. To use the window template, place the template shape desired over the fabric and move it around until you've isolated the part of the fabric you want to use. Draw around shape using fabric pen or pencil.

> ***Timely Tip:***
> For added interest and visual texture, sew together different fabrics to create the desired effect. Use the window template to isolate the area you want, then trace shape, **Fig 11**. This technique is especially useful for leaves to give a shaded effect.

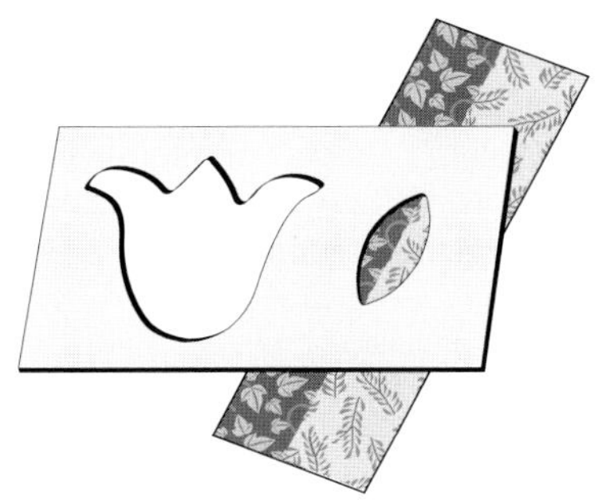

Fig 11

Embroidered, Stenciled and Pen-drawn Details

Some of the smaller details in the photographed blocks are created by stenciling, embroidery or drawing with a permanent fabric pen.

The bird eyes and beaks are all stenciled. Trace the small detail onto the dull side of freezer paper and cut out the detail with a craft knife. Use a brush or sponge to apply a permanent and safe fabric dye or paint through the stencil, **Fig 12**.

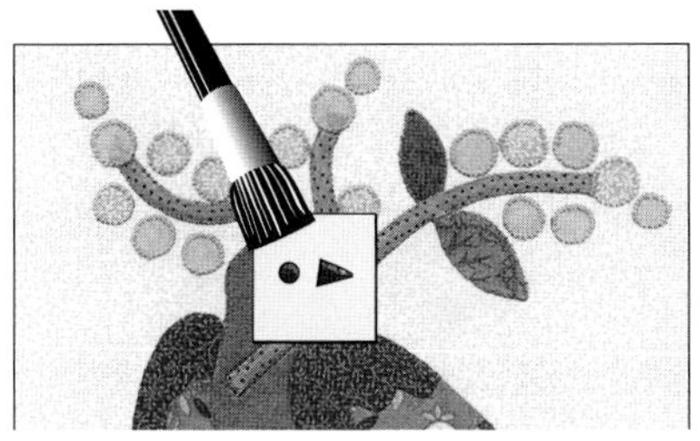

Fig 12

Practice the technique before trying it on a finished block.

Several block leaves have added stenciled details. Place a straight edge piece of cardboard over one half of the leaf and brush paint over the other half of the leaf, **Fig 13**.

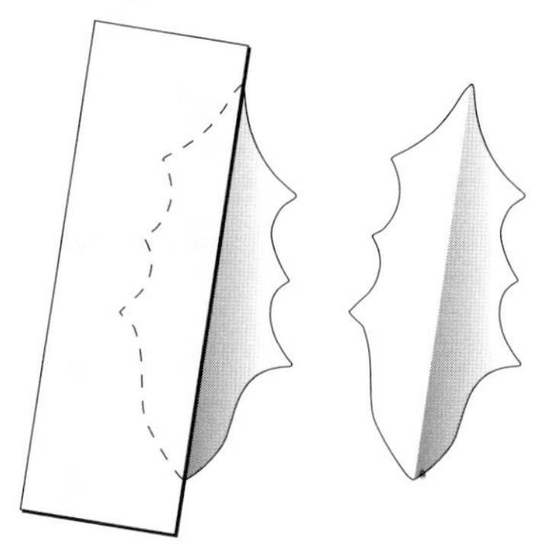

Fig 13

In addition to stenciling, small details such as stems and seeds can be added with a permanent fabric marker or the following embroidery stitches.

Embroidery Stitches

Chain Stitch

Use for stems, **Fig 14**.

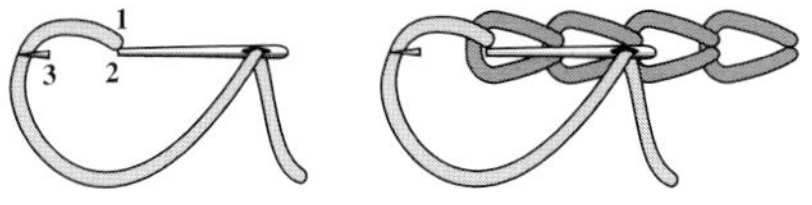

Fig 14

Lazy Daisy

Use for tiny leaves, **Fig 15.**

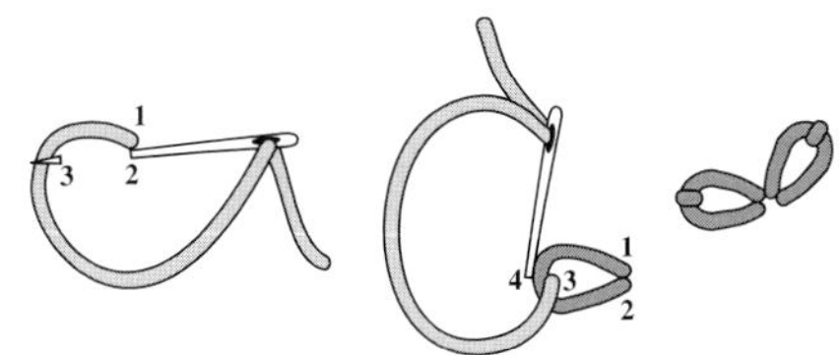

Fig 15

French Knot

Use for eyes or seeds, **Fig 16.**

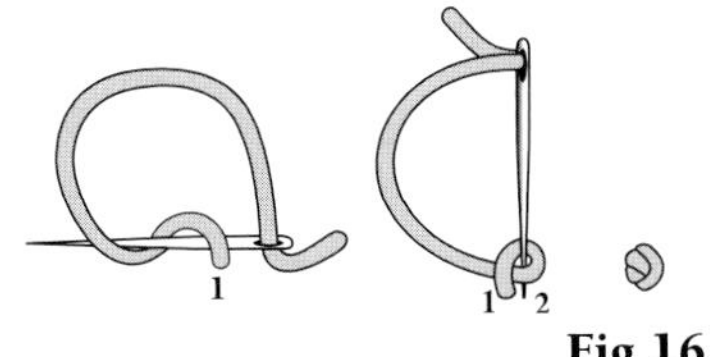

Fig 16

Stem Stitch

Use for thin stems or stamens, **Fig 17.**

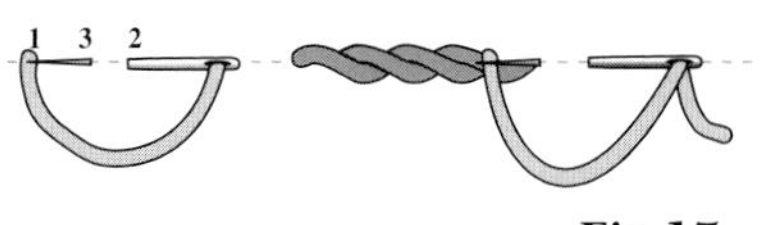

Fig 17

Preparing the Appliqué for Stitching

Cut background fabric to the size required for your block. The block designs in this book are made for a background size of 9½" (9" finished).

> ***Timely Tip:***
> Make a template the exact size of the finished block (9" for our patterns). Using this template, and a fabric marker, outline block on wrong side of background fabric. Cut out block allowing a ¼" seam allowance from marked edges.

Press or lightly mark centering lines on the background fabric, **Fig 18**.

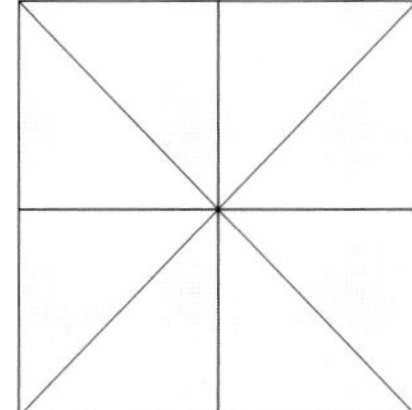

Fig 18

Making an Overlay

Place a piece of clear plastic or a plastic sheet protector over the appliqué design. Tape plastic to design to prevent slipping. Trace design onto plastic using a permanent marking pen, **Fig 19**.

Fig 19

Using the Overlay

Pin marked overlay to prepared background fabric. Use a ruler to make sure sides of design are of equal distance from edges of block. Set aside until appliqué pieces have been prepared.

How to Appliqué

There are many good techniques for hand and machine appliqué. The two techniques, Freezer Paper and Fabric Fusing (described in the following section) are suitable for any of the patterns.

Freezer Paper Technique

The freezer paper technique is useful for both hand and machine appliqué. It is easy to learn and use for most appliqué shapes. This technique was used for turning all but the smallest shapes in the photographed blocks.

1. Make cardboard templates needed for your block referring to Making and Using Templates, page 2.
2. Trace around template onto dull side of freezer paper.
3. Cut shape from paper. Do not include a seam allowance.

> ***Timely Tip:***
>
> DRAW ONCE–CUT MANY! For several of the same symmetrical shape, cut a strip of freezer paper the general height of the appliqué template. Draw shape onto dull side of paper. Accordion-fold the paper to fit the piece. Staple the folded paper together to keep it from slipping, **Fig 20**.

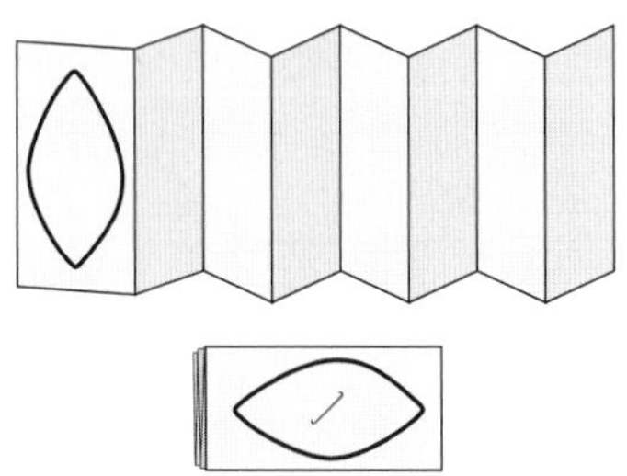

Fig 20

Cut out shape. ***Hint:*** Leave shapes stapled together and pull one off the back when needed.

4. Pin freezer paper piece to wrong side of fabric with the dull side down. Using a sharp hard pencil or stylus, trace around template to crease seam allowance fold line. Cut fabric around shape leaving a 1/4" seam allowance.
5. Clip inside curves and "V" areas almost to creased line, **Fig 21**. Clip as little as possible and never clip along outside curves.

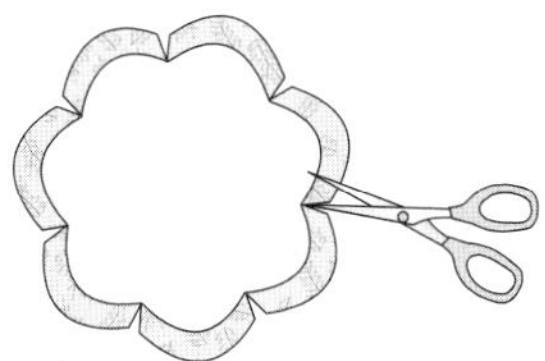

Fig 21

6. With tip-point of a hot iron, press seam allowance over edge of paper. Heat will cause seam allowance to stick to shiny side of freezer paper. Move along seam allowance edge carefully to create smooth curves and crisp points, **Fig 22.**

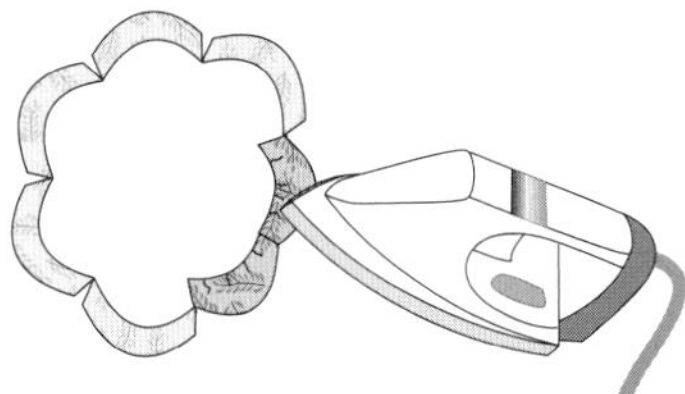

Fig 22

Place prepared pieces in a plastic bag to protect them until they are ready to use. If the shape is very complicated, or you do not plan to use it soon, you may want to thread or glue baste the edges down.

> ***Timely Tip:***
>
> Use a smaller lightweight travel iron to press seam allowances to freezer paper. The smaller iron makes it easier to control the delicate edges of the appliqué.

7. Place prepared background square on flat surface. Slip prepared appliqué pieces under overlay and position according to drawing. Remove overlay and press motifs; freezer paper will adhere to background. Baste pieces by hand or machine.
8. Appliqué pieces by hand or machine, referring to Appliqué Stitches, pages 3 and 4. Turn to underside and cut away background fabric under appliqué pieces, leaving a 1/4" seam allowance, **Fig 23**. Remove freezer paper through opening.

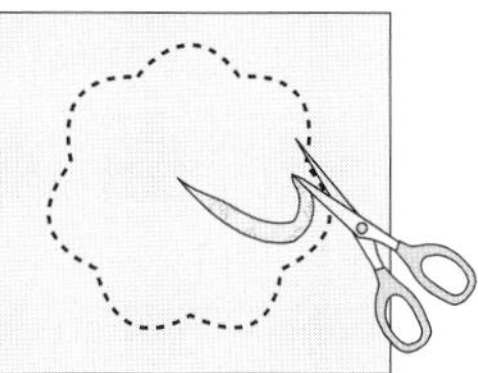

Fig 23

Fabric Fusing Technique

The fabric fusing technique allows you to quickly appliqué even very complicated shapes. Do not include the seam allowances when calculating fabric requirements. Some of the smaller leaves and all of the small circles in the photographed blocks were applied using a medium-weight fusible webbing and overstitched with a small close blanket stitch.

Fabric fusing products are sold by the yard or on a roll in stores selling fabric. These paper-backed products are available in various weights and strengths (holding power). Read and follow the manufacturer's instructions. Keep the original instructions with any leftover product as they differ widely from manufacturer to manufacturer.

Using Fusing Products

1. On the paper side of fusible web, trace around actual-size appliqué template. Place template with labeled side down or your piece will end up being a mirror image. Trace the number of pieces you need, keeping pieces of the same "fabric color family" very close to each other on the paper, **Fig 24**.

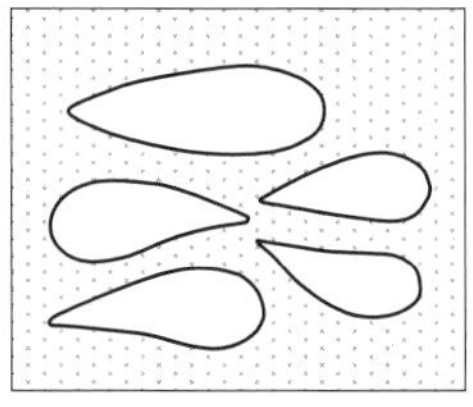

Fig 24

2. Rough-cut the color family block from the fusible web.
3. Place marked fusible web onto wrong side of chosen fabric.
   Note: The paper side must be facing you and the iron, with the fusible side facing wrong side of fabric.
4. First, tack the fusible web onto fabric by touching iron to fabric in a few spots; then, iron from center toward edges. Do not remove paper backing at this time. ***Note***: Follow manufacturer's directions for fusing.
5. Cut each shape from fused fabric along traced outlines. Remove paper backing only when you are ready to use a piece.
6. Place prepared background right side up on a flat surface. Arrange appliqué pieces face up between overlay and background. Remove overlay and fuse in place, following manufacturer's instructions.

Timely Tips:

Protect your ironing board from fabric fusing products. Place a piece of typing paper between fusible pieces and iron.

There are products on the market that remove the adhesive from your iron–in case you ever forget which side goes down. I know from experience that it can really make a mess of your iron.

Keep the fused fabric pieces away from sunlight and heat. Otherwise, they will fuse together into a useless blob.

Some Special Techniques

Appliqué is very forgiving as a technique, but there are a few firm guidelines to follow–circles should be smooth, pointed leaves should remain pointed and stems and vines should be of even width and appear to move gracefully.

The good thing about these guidelines is that even a beginner can quickly learn the skills it takes to follow them.

Pointed Leaves

Using the Freezer Paper technique, press seam allowance over paper, **Fig 25**.

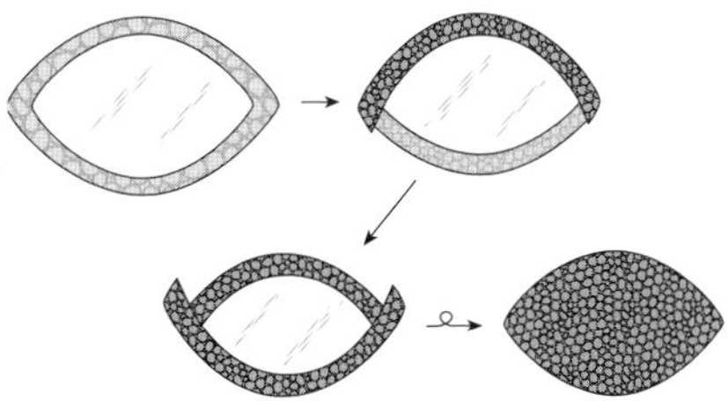

Fig 25

Do not cut off excess fabric tag at ends of leaf. Roll this tag of seam allowance fabric under the leaf just before you stitch it down. Use a wooden toothpick or a stylus.

Timely Tip: If a seam allowance does not want to remain stuck to the plastic backing of the freezer paper, put a dab of glue stick on it.

Perfect Circles

Method 1. Pin freezer-paper circle, shiny side up, onto wrong side of fabric circle. Trim seam allowance to 1/8". Carefully press allowance over the freezer paper with a hot iron, **Fig 26**.

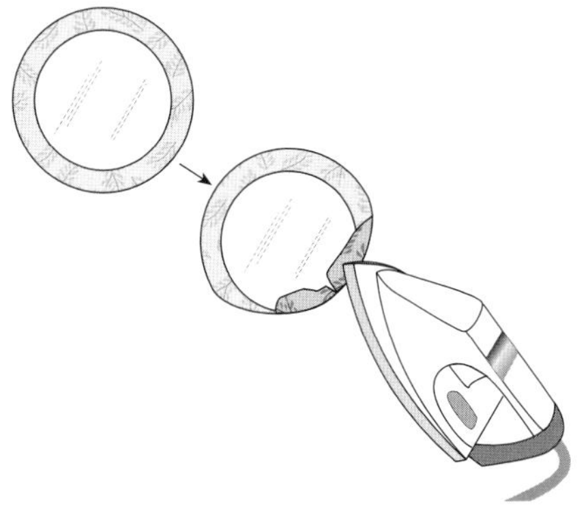

Fig 26

Method 2. Make fabric circle at least 1 1/8" larger than finished size of circle. Stitch 1/8" from outside edge of fabric circle. Place a paper template in center of fabric and draw up fabric around the template, **Fig 27**.

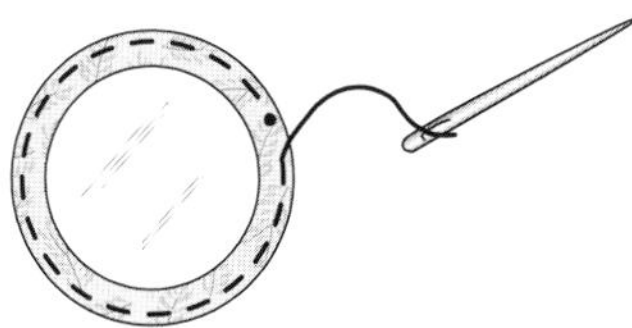

Fig 27

Make a knot. Press. Remove paper template after circle is stitched down.

Stacked Designs

Many appliqué patterns have multiple layers built up over just one foundation piece. Prairie Blossoms, Block #25, is one example of this type of pattern. Center smaller parts (with smallest on top) onto larger flower piece then appliqué composite flower onto background fabric, **Fig 28**.

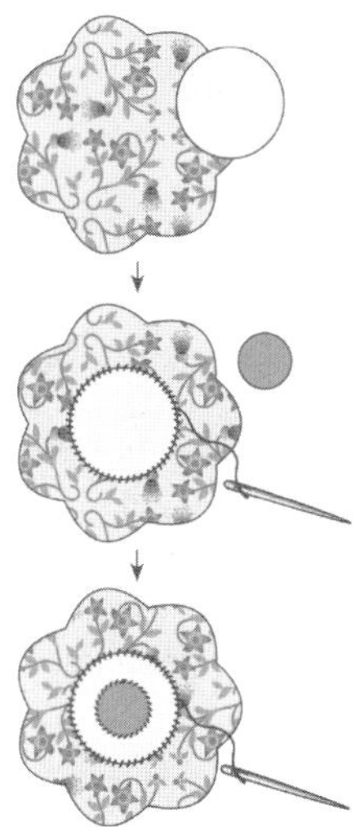

Fig 28

Reverse Appliqué

Reverse appliqué is a quick and easy way to apply detail into a design.

1. Trace pattern onto paper side of freezer paper. Cut out along outside edge, then cut out part(s) of design to be reverse appliquéd.
2. Use the Freezer Paper technique, page 6, to prepare the piece along outside edge, **Fig 29**.

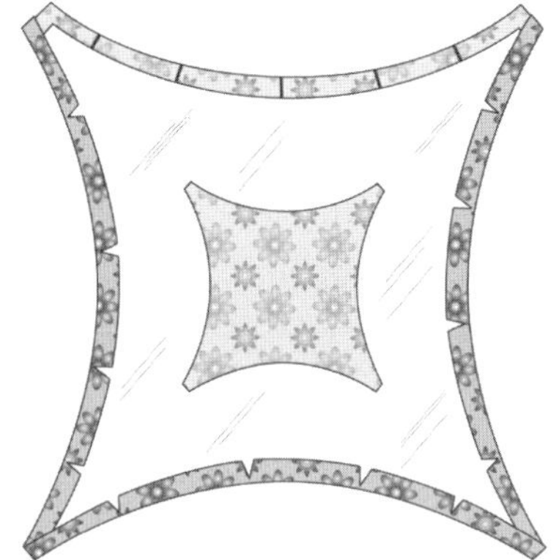

Fig 29

3. Next, remove fabric from area to be reversed, **Fig 30**, leaving at least a 1/4" seam allowance when possible.

Fig 30

4. Clip any inner fabric curves and "V" areas.
5. Iron seam allowance to freezer paper, **Fig 31**.

Fig 31

6. Place another piece of fabric, right side down on freezer paper, centered over opening, **Fig 32**. Tack in place with glue stick.

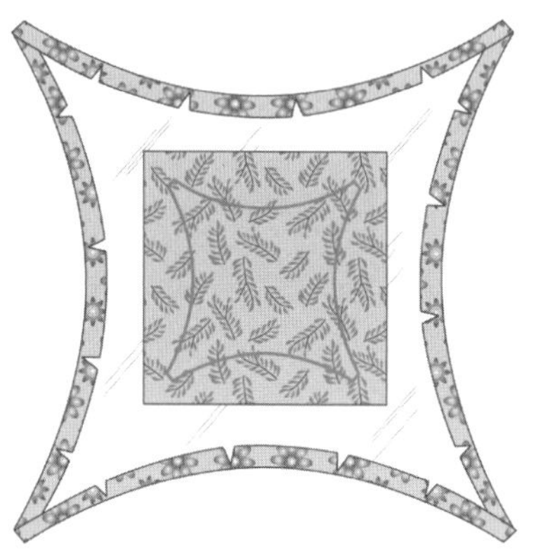

Fig 32

7. Appliqué edges by hand or machine, **Fig 33**.

Fig 33

Stems and Vines

It's easy to make flowing, flat, stems and vines with bias bars. The photographed blocks have stems made with 1/8", 3/16" and 1/4" metal bias bars. The bias strips were cut from fat quarters.

Making and Using Bias Strips

1. Fold a corner of the fabric over to make a 45° angle; finger press fold.
2. Open fabric and cut along fold, **Fig 34.**

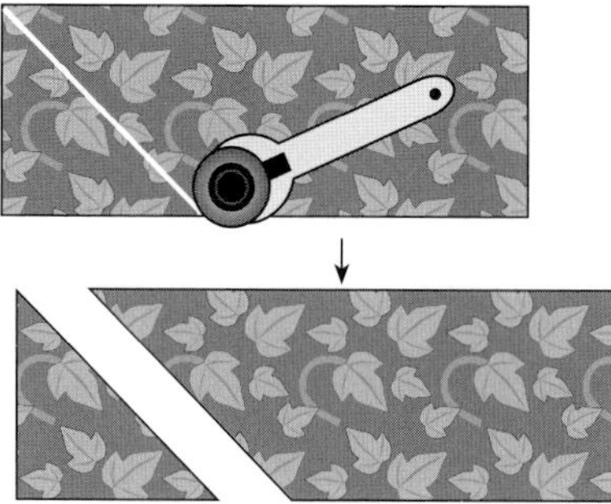

Fig 34

3. Determine width of bias strips needed following the bias bar manufacturer's guidelines for the width of strip you will need, then cut strips using first cut edge as a guide, **Fig 35**.

Fig 35

Timely Tip: You will need to experiment with the bias strip width. Your stitching habits will ultimately determine the size strips you will need to use.

4. Join cut strips to form a longer strip, sewing along short ends, **Fig 36.**

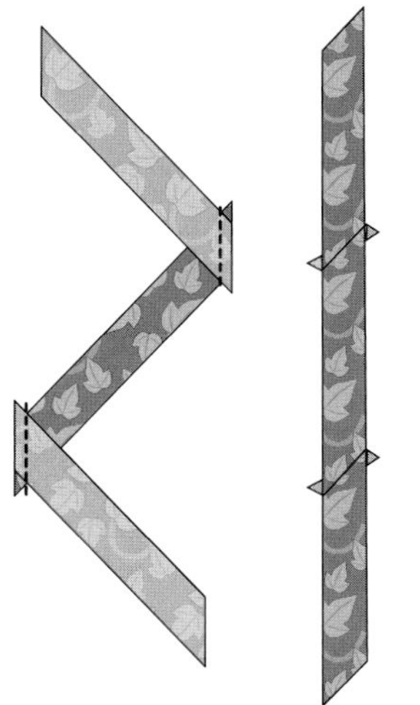

Fig 36

Using Bias Bars

Bias bars come in many widths from 1/8" to 1". Bias tubes are sewn from bias strips of fabric.

1. Press bias strip in half lengthwise with wrong sides together, then make a line of machine stitching two or three threads wider than the bias bar. This creates the bias tube, **Fig 37.**

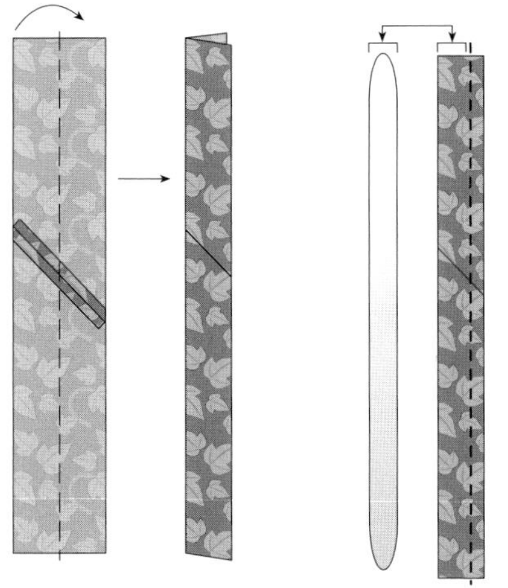

Fig 37

2. Trim excess fabric close to stitching. Place bias bar into tube and slip seam line around to underside of bar, **Fig 38.**

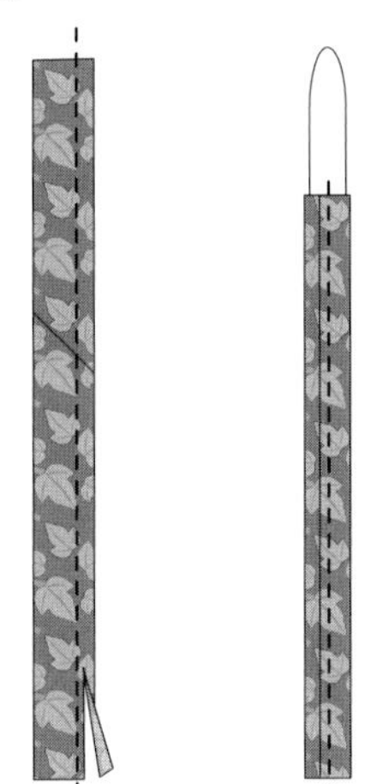

Fig 38

5. Spray-starch front of fabric and press with an iron. Slip bar further through fabric tube and continue pressing.
6. Wrap finished bias tube around an old spool or a piece of cardboard until you are ready to use it.

Planning the Quilt

You can place the block designs into any number of settings. The following settings are just a few of the many options.

Straight Set

Diagonal Set

Skip Block

Sashing with Cornerstones

Streak of Lightning

1

Classic Whig Rose

Special Notes:
Use 1/8" bias bar for stems; reverse appliqué center.

Dragonfly's Delight

2

Special Notes:
Use 3/16" bias bar for stem; draw antennae with permanent fabric marker.

3 Autumn Wreath

Special Note:
Use 1/4" bias bar for stem.

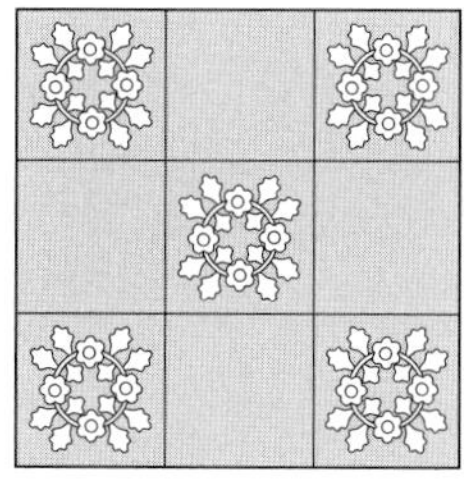

Butterfly in Hand

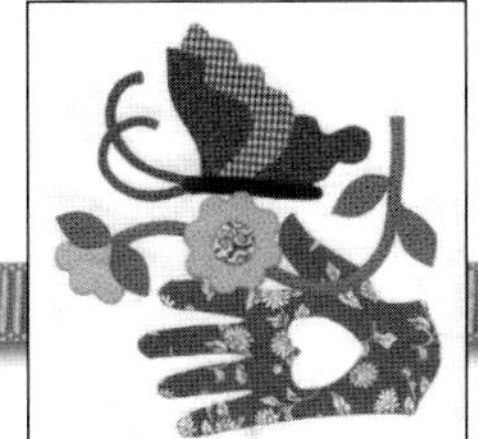

4

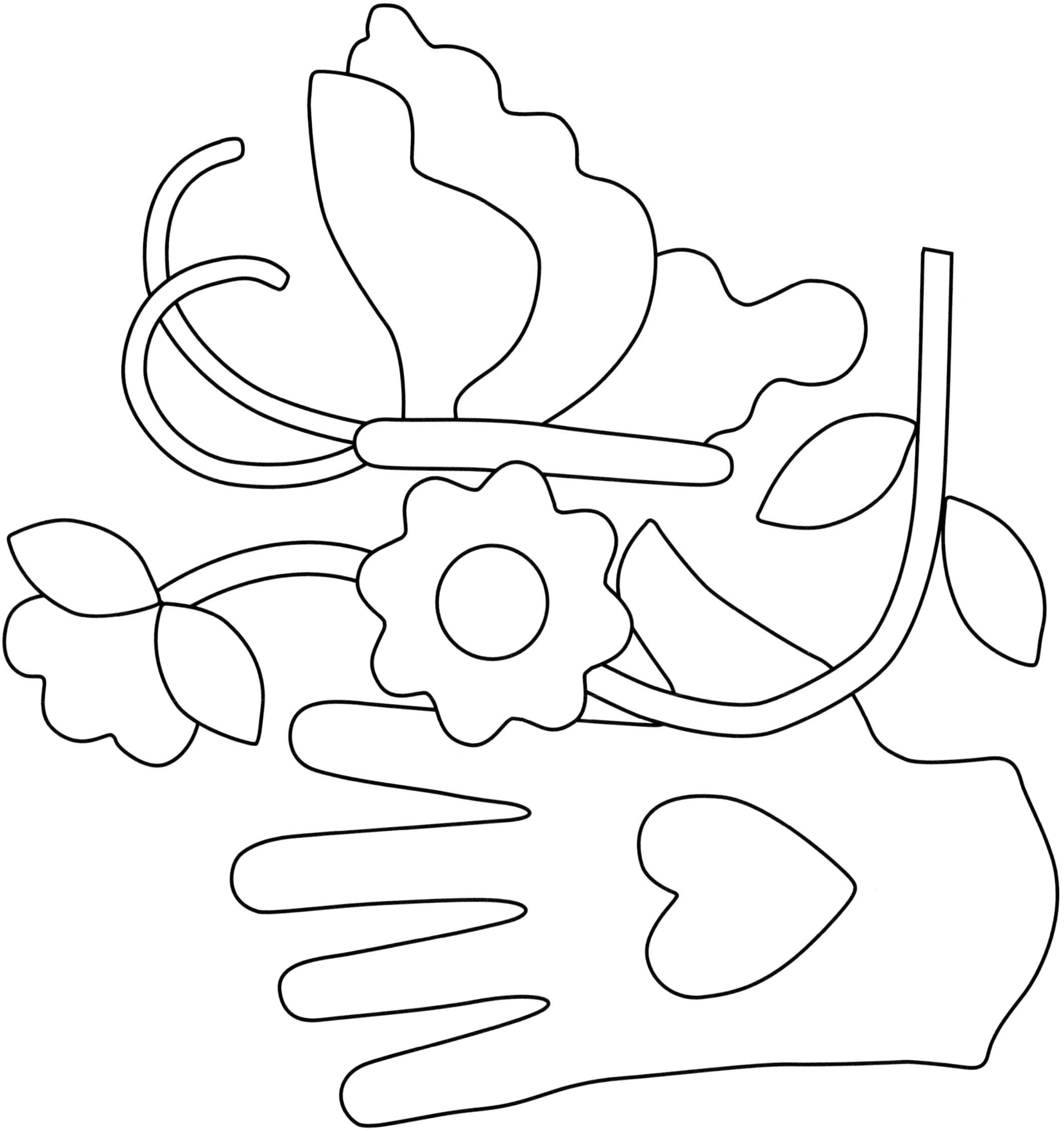

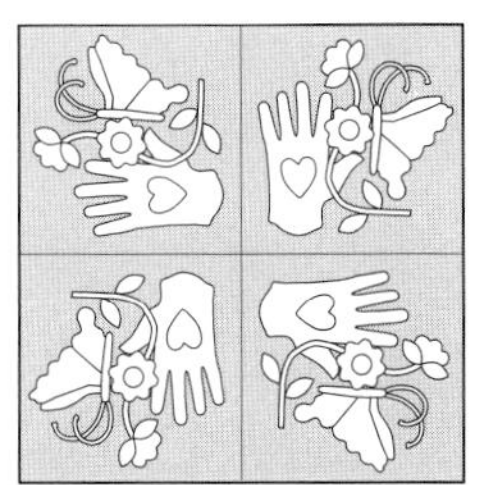

Special Notes:
Use 3/16" bias bar for stem and 1/8" bias bar for antennae; reverse appliqué heart.

5 

Urn and Flowers

Special Note:
Use 3/16" bias bar for stems.

Spring Promises

6

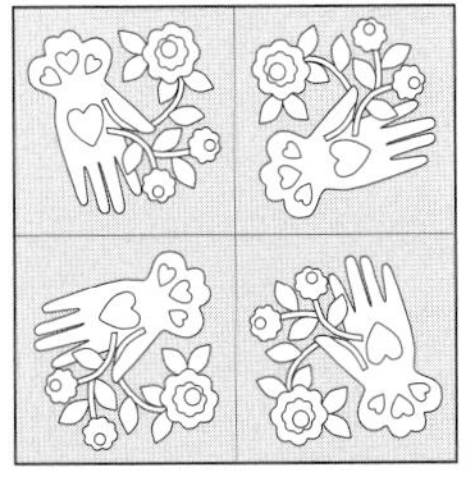

Special Notes:
Use 1/4" bias bar for stems; reverse appliqué hearts.

7

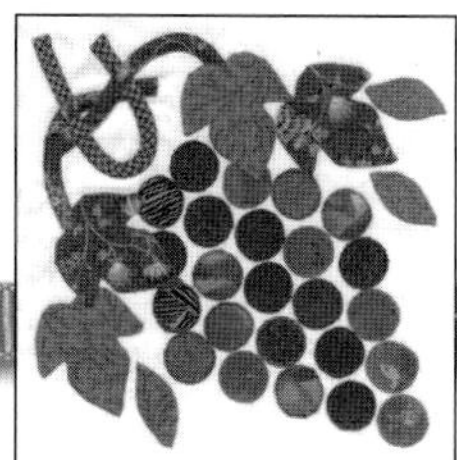

Grape Cluster

Special Note:
Use 1/4" bias bar for stems.

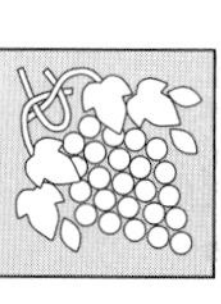

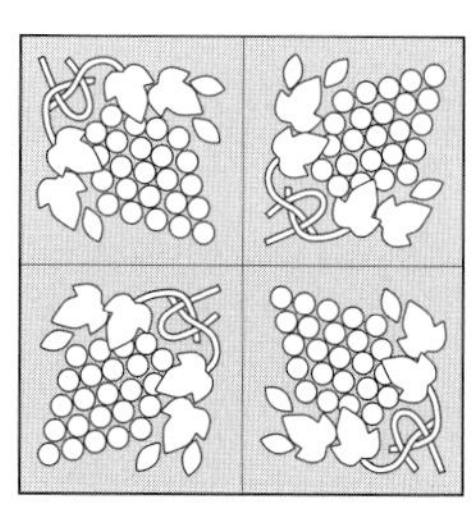

Grape Spray

8

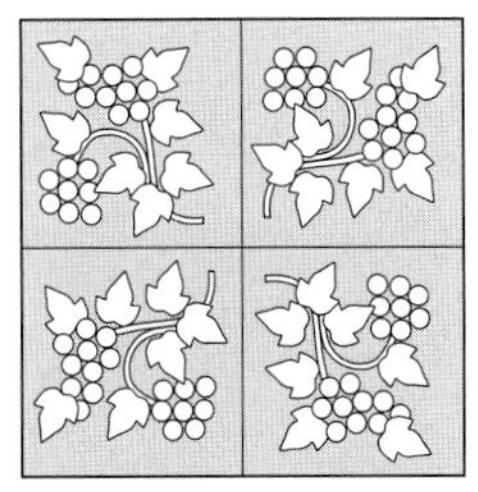

Special Note:
Use 1/4" bias bar for stems.

9

Grape Wreath

Special Note:
Use 1/4" bias bar for stems.

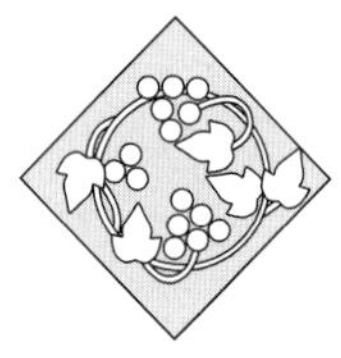

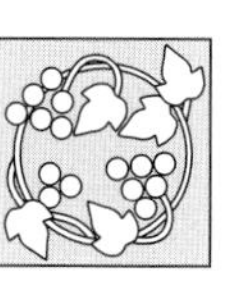

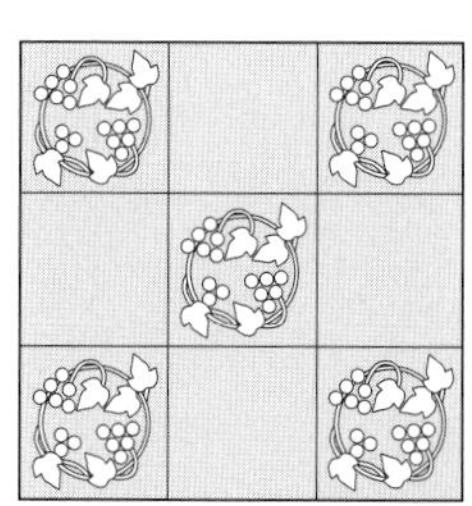

Bird in a Berry Bush

10

Special Notes:
Use 1/4" bias bar for stems; stencil details in eye and beak.

11 Hearts and Hands

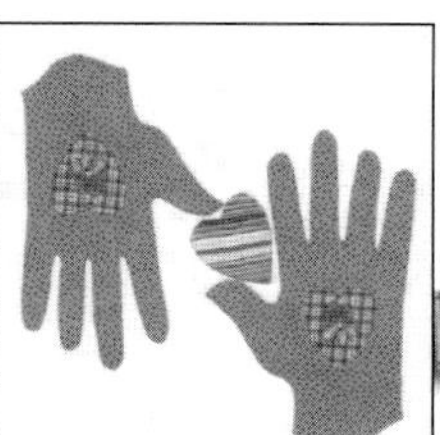

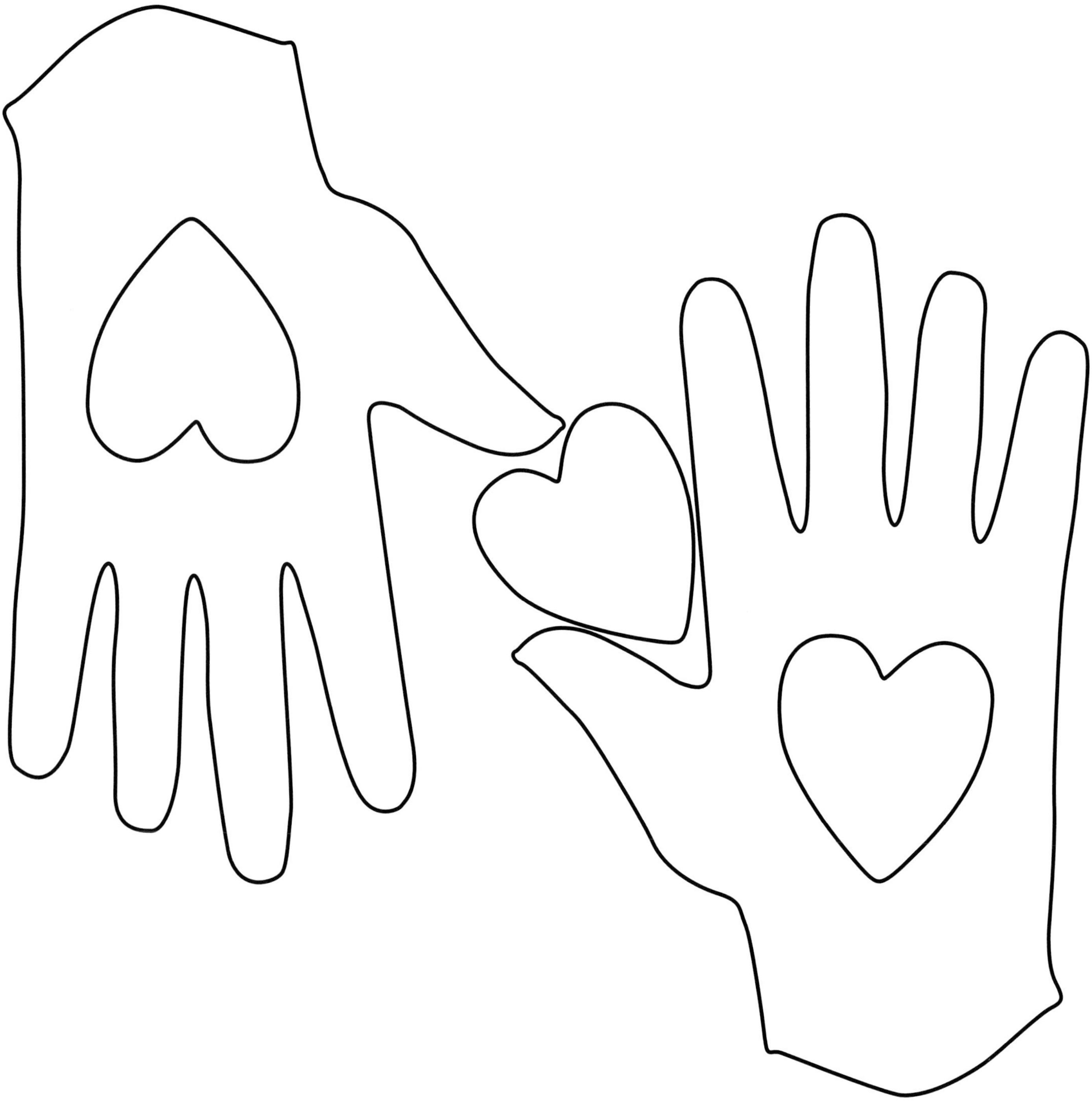

Special Note:
Reverse appliqué
hearts on hands.

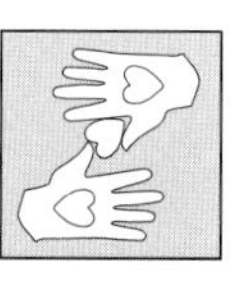

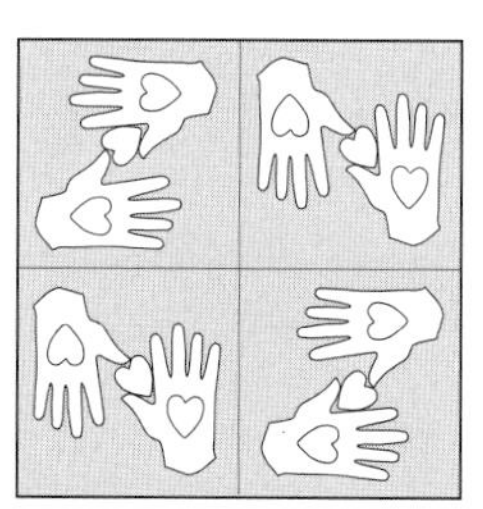

Stylized Flower Stem

12

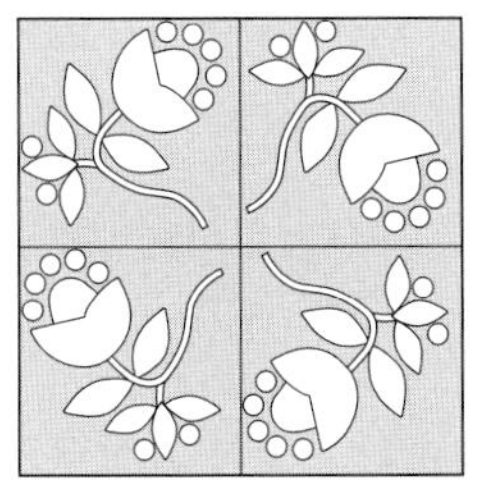

Special Note:
Use 1/4" bias bar for stems.

13 

Windblown Wildflowers

Special Note:
Use 3/16" bias bar for stems.

Fanciful Butterfly

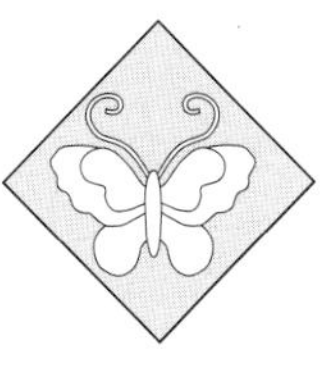

Special Note:
Use 1/8" bias bar for antennae.

15 Twin Tulips

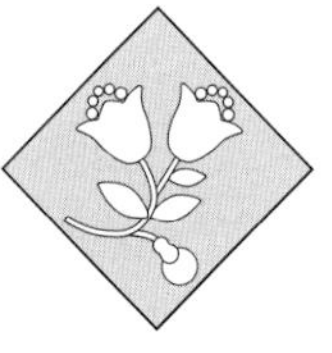

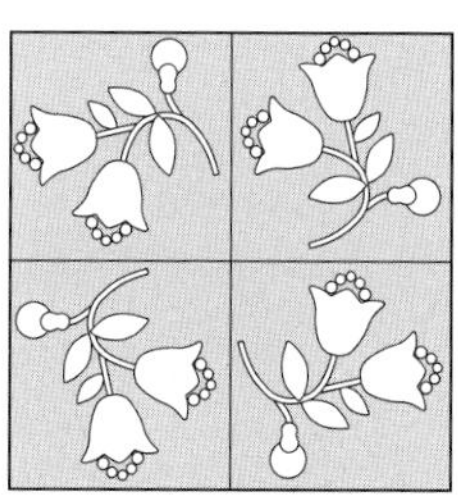

Special Note:
Use 1/4" bias bar for stems.

Special Note:
Use 1/4" bias bar for stems.

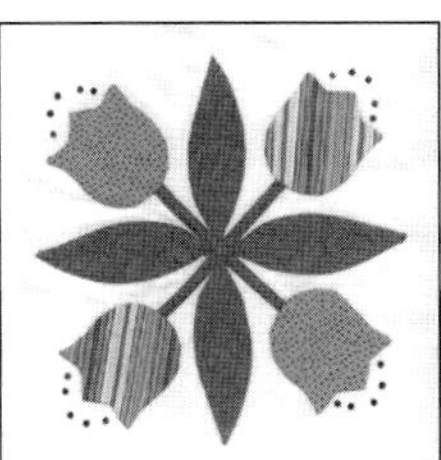

Crossed Tulips

Special Notes:
Use 1/4" bias bar for stems; stencil flower details.

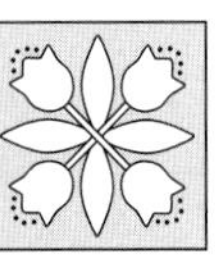

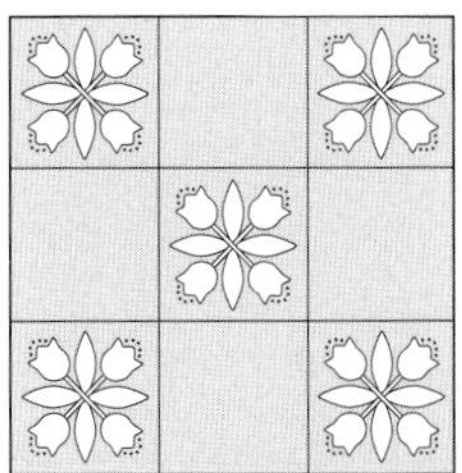

Whimsical Butterfly

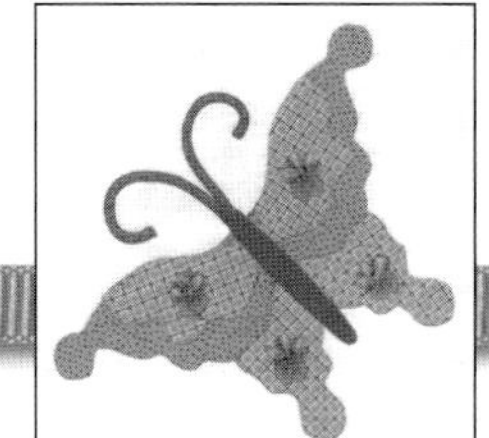

18

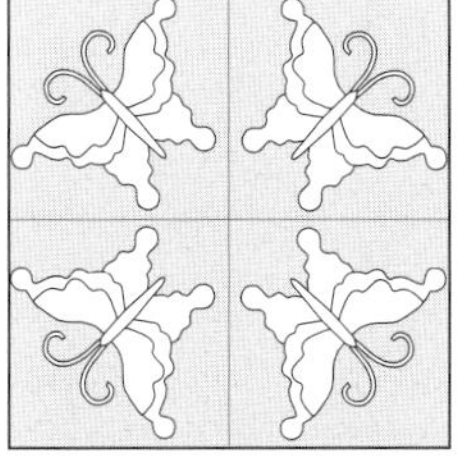

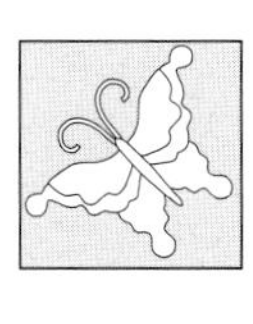

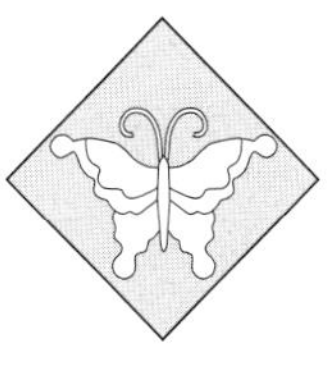

Special Note:
Use 1/8" bias bar for antennae.

19

Formal Bouquet

Special Notes:
Use 1/4" bias bar for stems; stencil detail in leaves.

Twining Buds

20

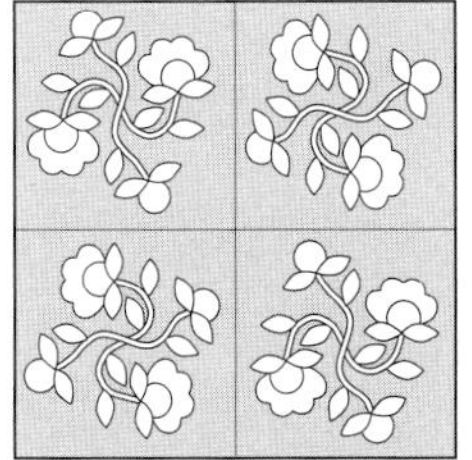

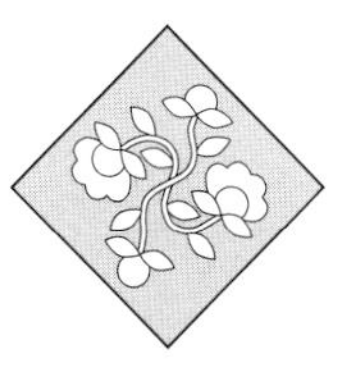

Special Note:
Use 1/4" bias bar for stems.

21 

Dancing Currants

Special Note:
Use 1/4" bias bar for stems.

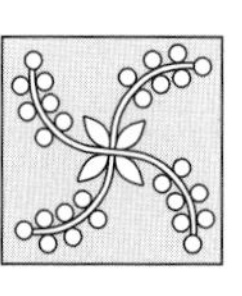

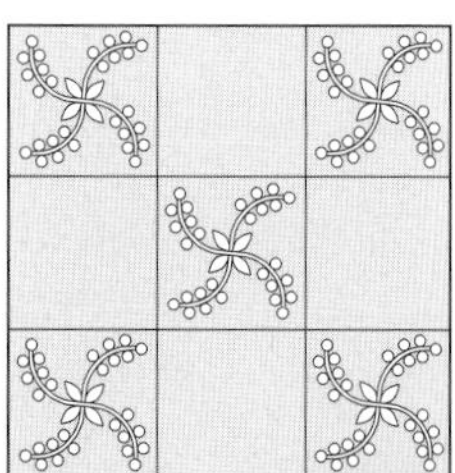

Mystical Moth

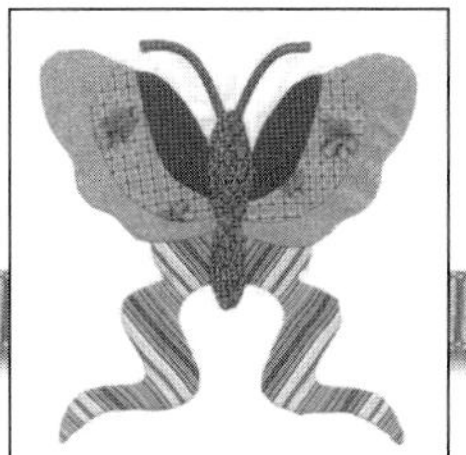

22

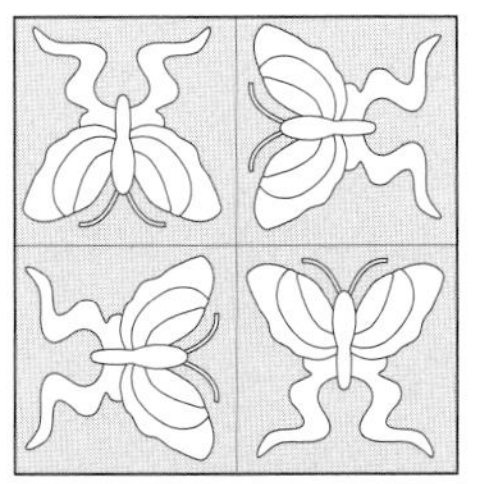

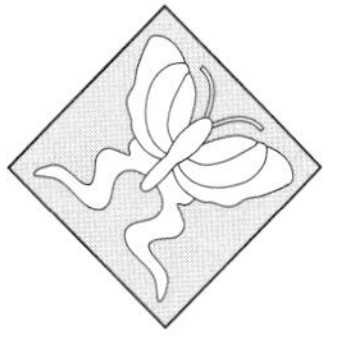

Special Note:
Use 1/8" bias bar for antennae.

23 Miniature Rose Wreath

Special Note:
Use 1/4" bias bar for stem.

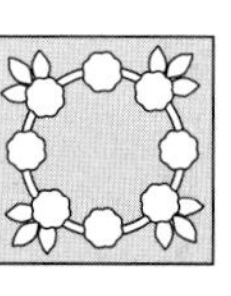

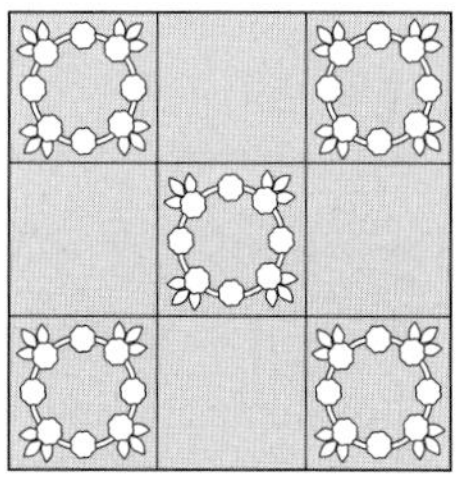

Berry Sprigs

24

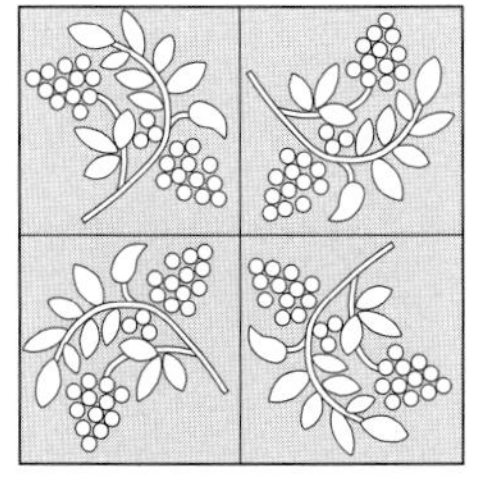

Special Note:
Use 1/4" bias bar for stems.

25  Prairie Blossoms

Special Note:
Use 1/4" bias bar for stems.

Prairie Garden

26

Special Note:
Use 1/4" bias bar for stems.

27 Butterfly and Flower Flourish

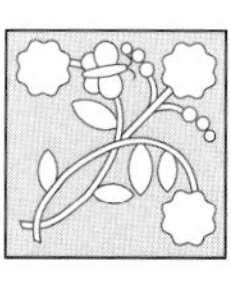

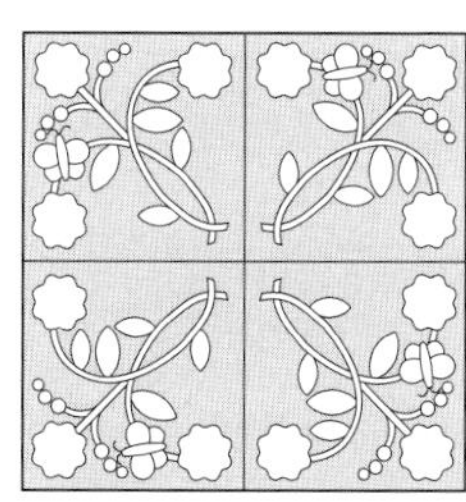

Special Notes:
Use 1/4" bias bar for stems; chain stitch for antennae.

Special Notes:
Reverse appliqué center and each leaf detail; use permanent fabric marker for writing.

29 Butterfly Wreath

Special Notes:
Use 1/4" bias bar for stem; chain stitch antennae.

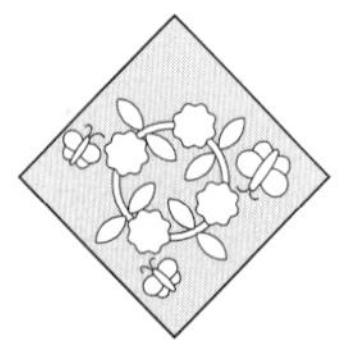

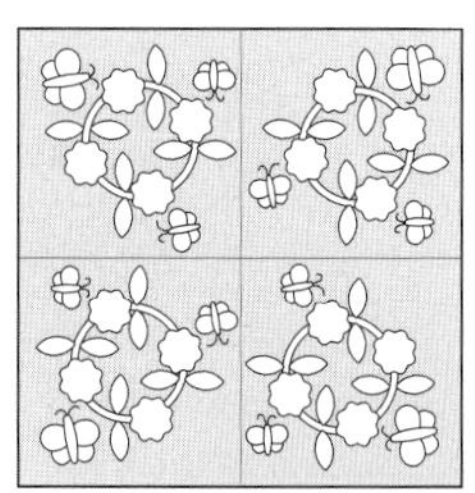

Thistle Pot

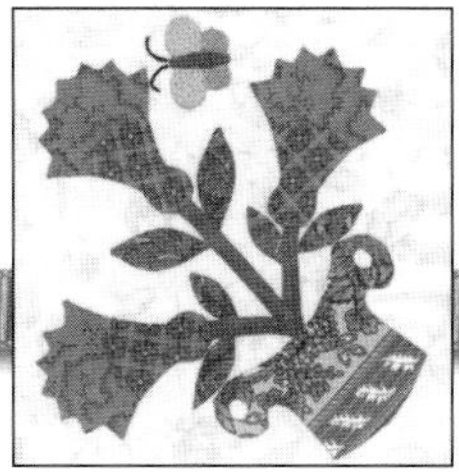

30

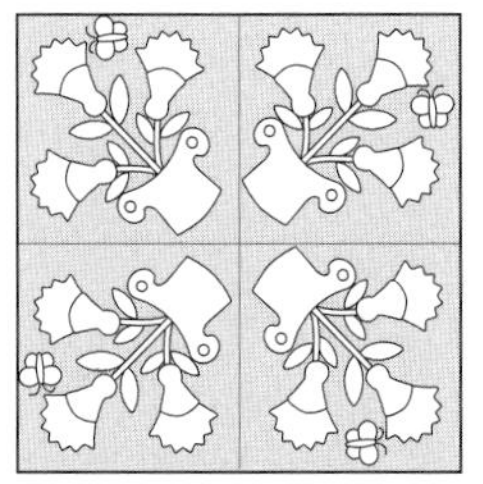

Special Notes:
Use 1/4" bias bar for stems; reverse appliqué handle details; chain stitch antennae.

31 

Crossed Stems

Special Note:
Use 1/4" bias bar for stems.

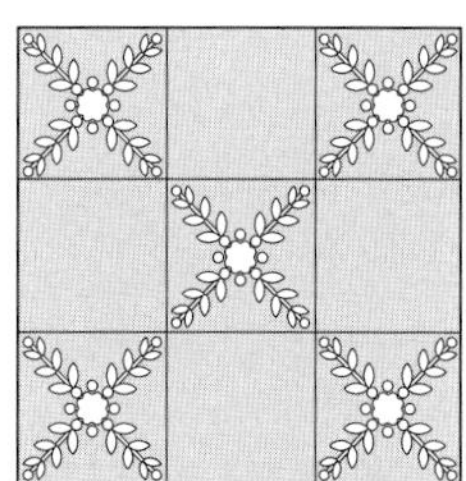

Special Note:
Use 1/4" bias bar for stems.

33

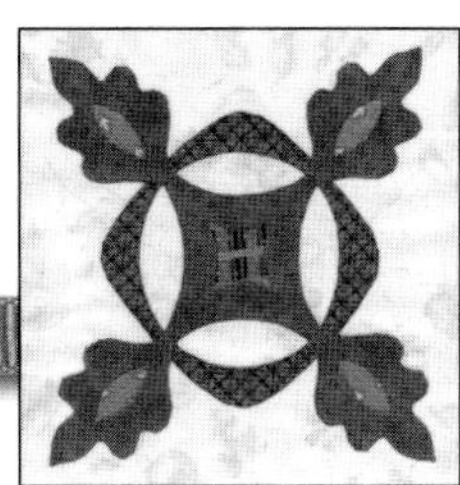

Oak Leaf and Reel

Special Notes:
Reverse appliqué center and in each leaf.

Double Swag Rose

34

Special Note:
Use 1/4" bias bar for stems.

35 Heart in Star

Special Note:
Reverse appliqué heart.

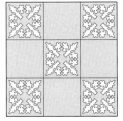

Forest Floor

36

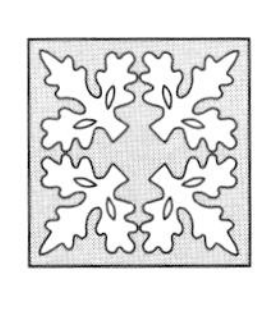

Special Note:
Reverse appliqué on leaves.

37

Bird in a Cherry Tree

Special Notes:
Use 1/4" bias bar for stems; chain stitch cherry stems, Lazy Daisy for cherry leaves, French Knot for eye; reverse appliqué heart.

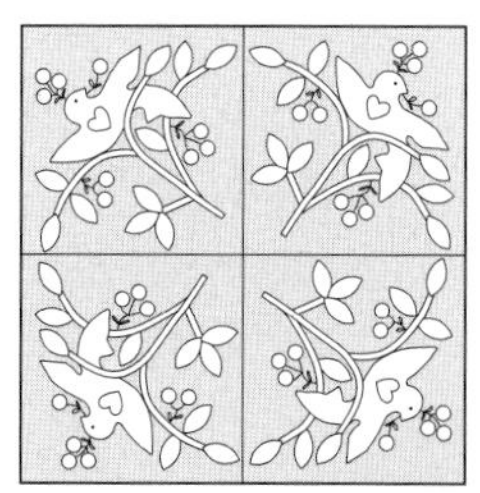

Double Star and Currants

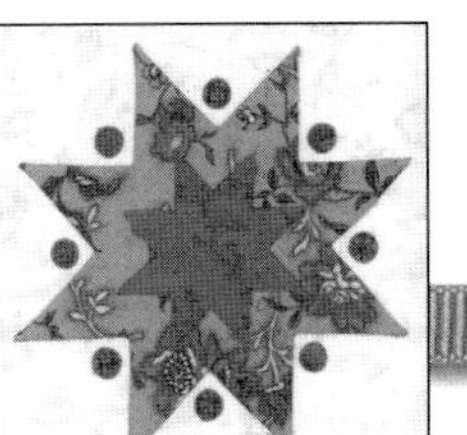

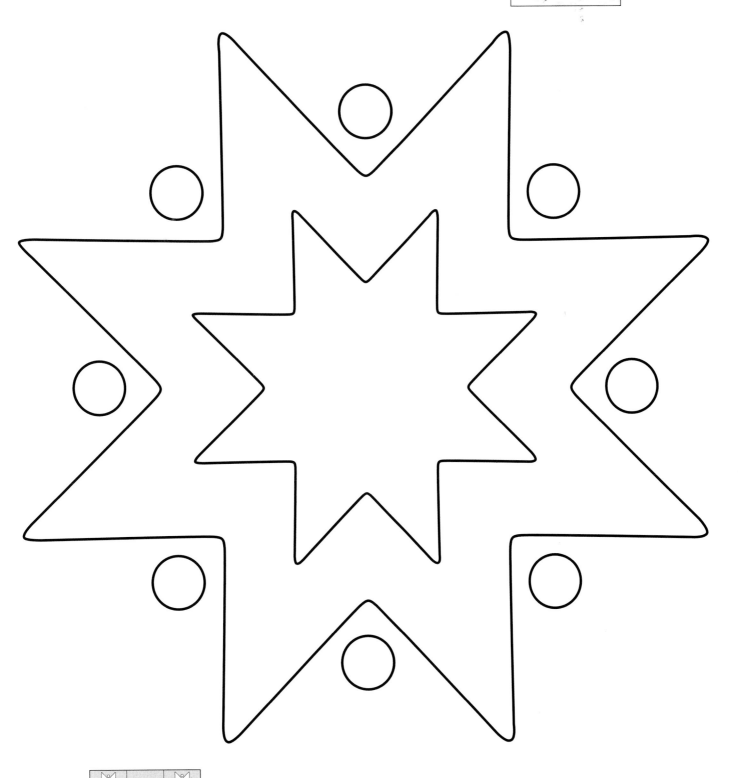

Special Note:
Reverse appliqué center star.

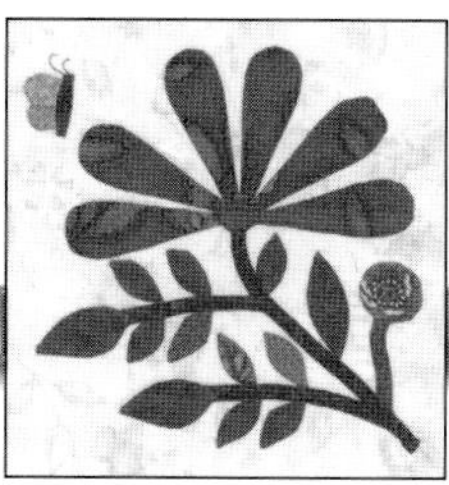

Fan Flower

Special Notes:
Use 1/4" bias bar for stems; use permanent fabric marker for antennae.

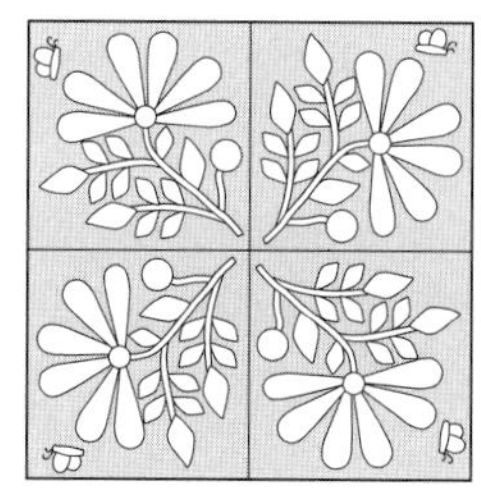

Cardinal's Fancy

40

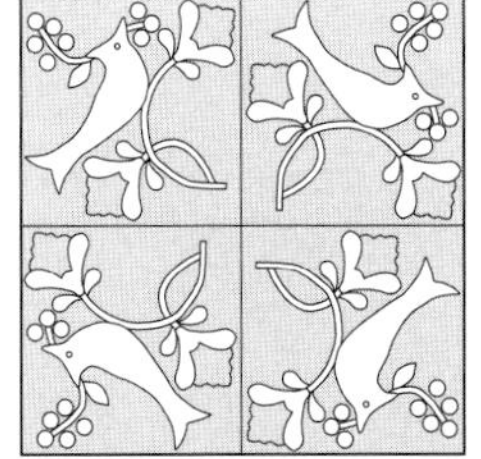

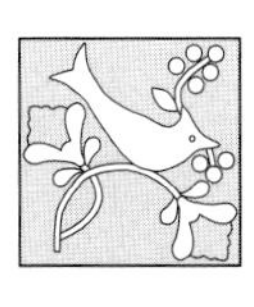

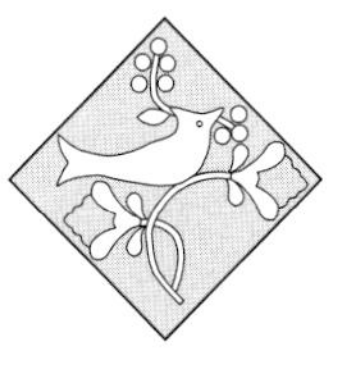

Special Notes:
Use 1/4" bias bar for stems; for beak, sew black beak fabric to red body fabric; make a window template to cut out bird (see page 5).

41 Poinsettia Display

Special Note:
Use 1/4" bias bar for stems.

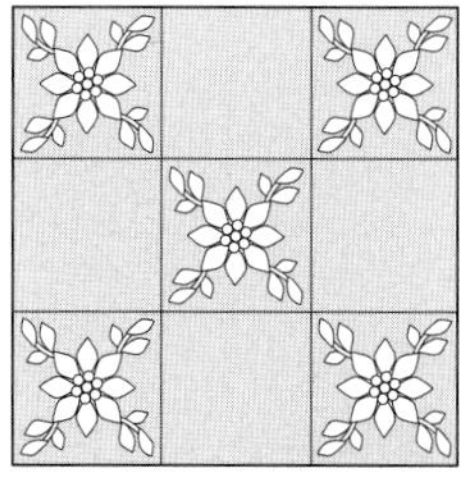

Brimming Basket

42

Special Note:
Use 1/4" bias bar for stems.

43

Fan Flower Spray

Special Note:
Use 1/4" bias bar for stems.

Bird in a Peony Bush

44

Special Notes:
Use 3/16" bias bar for stems; stencil eye and beak.

45

Peony Bouquet

Special Note:
Use 1/4" bias bar for stems.

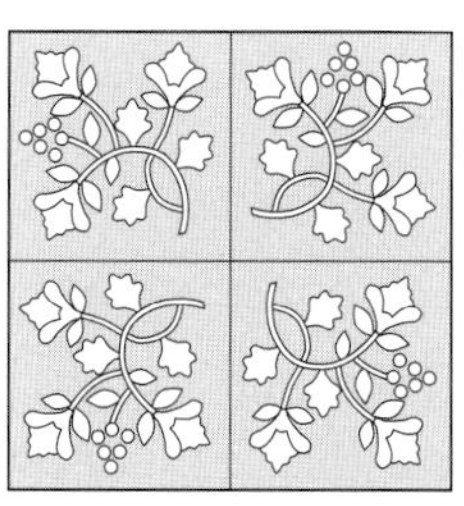

Formal Flower Wreath

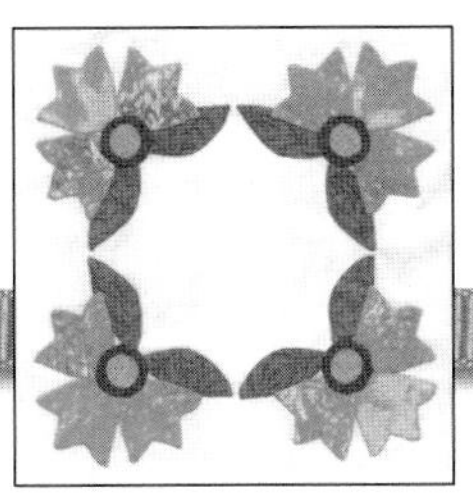

46

47

Radiant Wildflower

4
5
6
8
9
10
12
13
14
16
17
18
20
21
22

23 - 42

23
24
25
26
27
28
When This You See Remember Me
29
30
31
32
33
34
35
36
37
38
39
40
41
42

43 - 62
43
44
45
46
47
48
49
50
51
52
53
54
55
56
57
58
59
60
61
62

63 - 82

Sunny Flowers

48

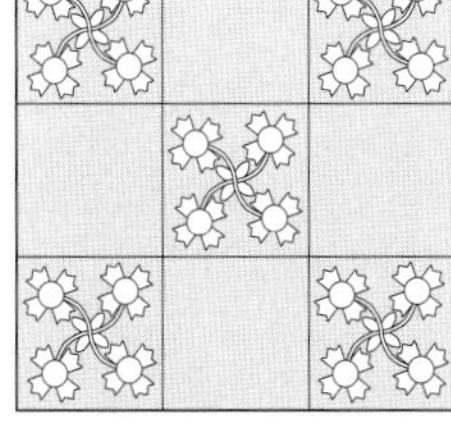

Special Note:
Use 3/16" bias bar for stems.

Buttercup Spray

Special Note:
Use 1/4" bias bar for stems.

Modern Star Flower

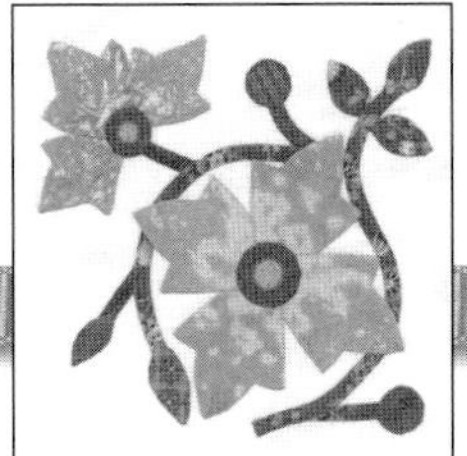

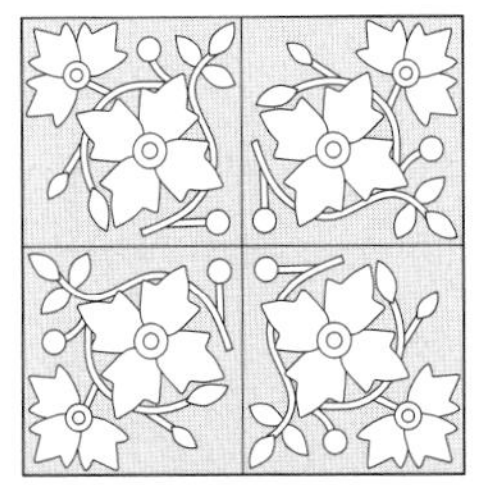

Special Note:
Use 1/4" bias bar for stems.

51 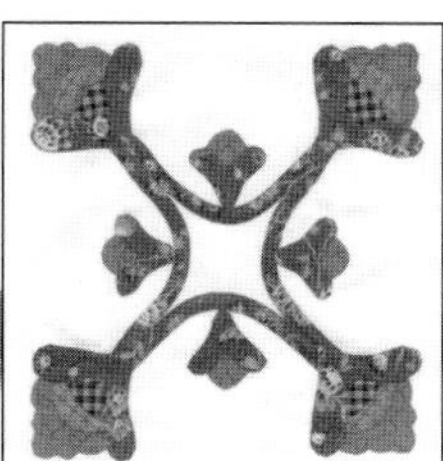

Formal Peony

Special Note:
Use 1/4" bias bar for stems.

Mexican Sunflower

Special Note:
Use 3/16" bias bar for stems.

53 Swirling Posies

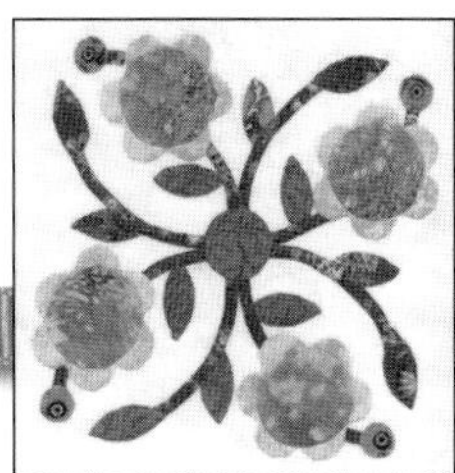

Special Note:
Use 3/16" bias bar for stems.

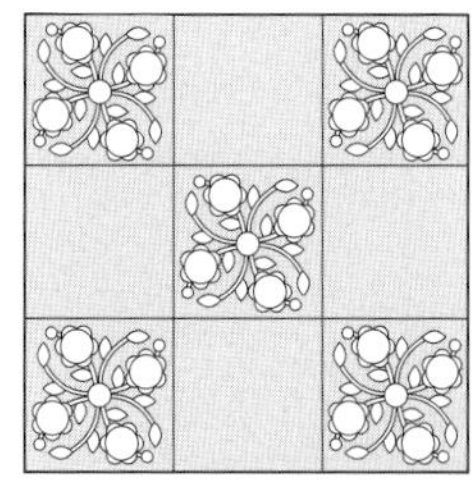

Old Fashioned Rose

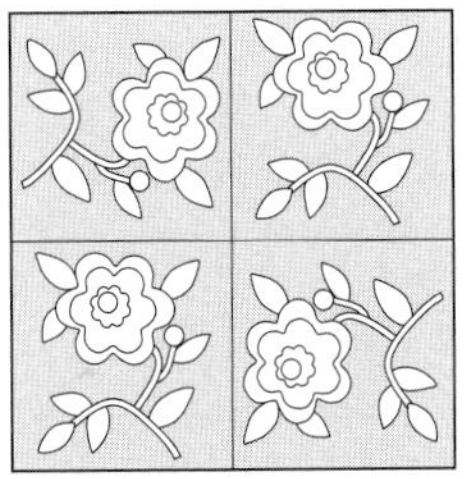

Special Note:
Use 1/4" bias bar for stems.

55 Natural Sunflowers

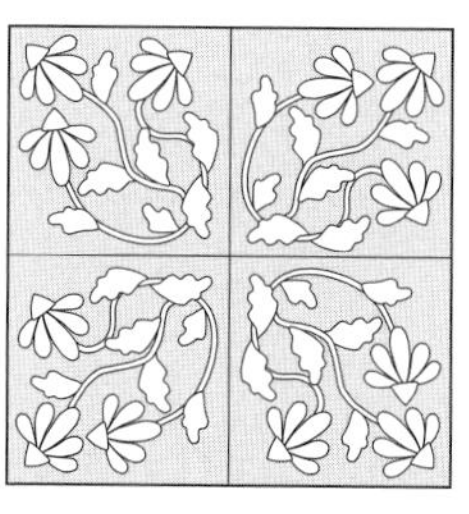

Special Note:
Use 3/16" bias bar for stems.

Pride of the Forest

56

Special Note:
Reverse appliqué in leaves.

57 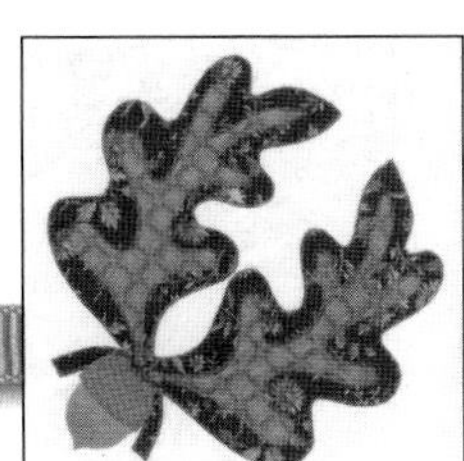

Curved Oak Leaves

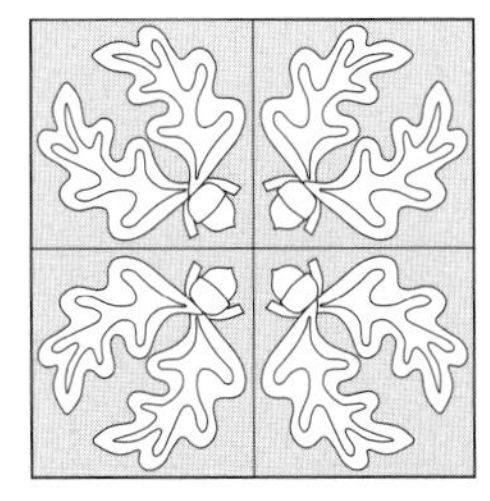

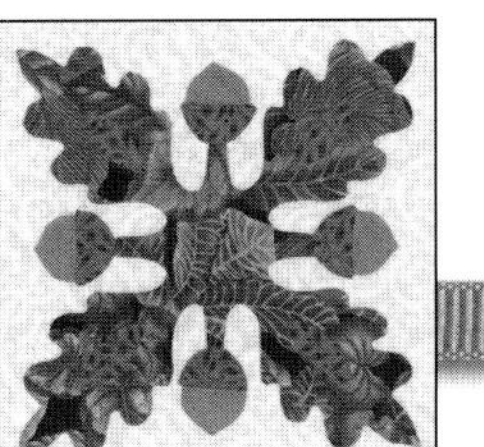

Special Note:
Reverse appliqué in leaves.

59 

Oak Wreath

Special Notes:
Use 1/4" bias bar for stems; reverse appliqué in leaves.

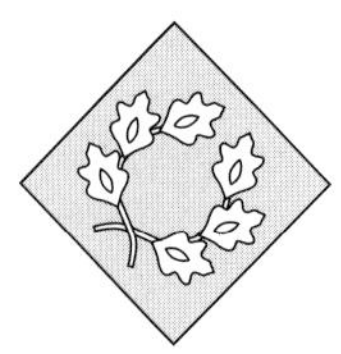

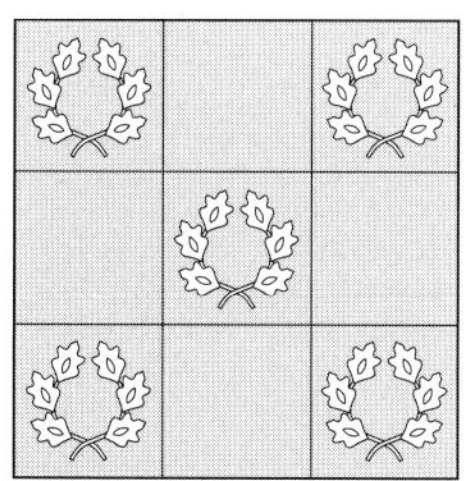

Oak Leaf Medley

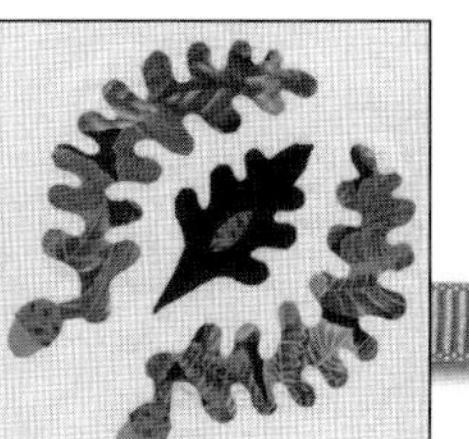

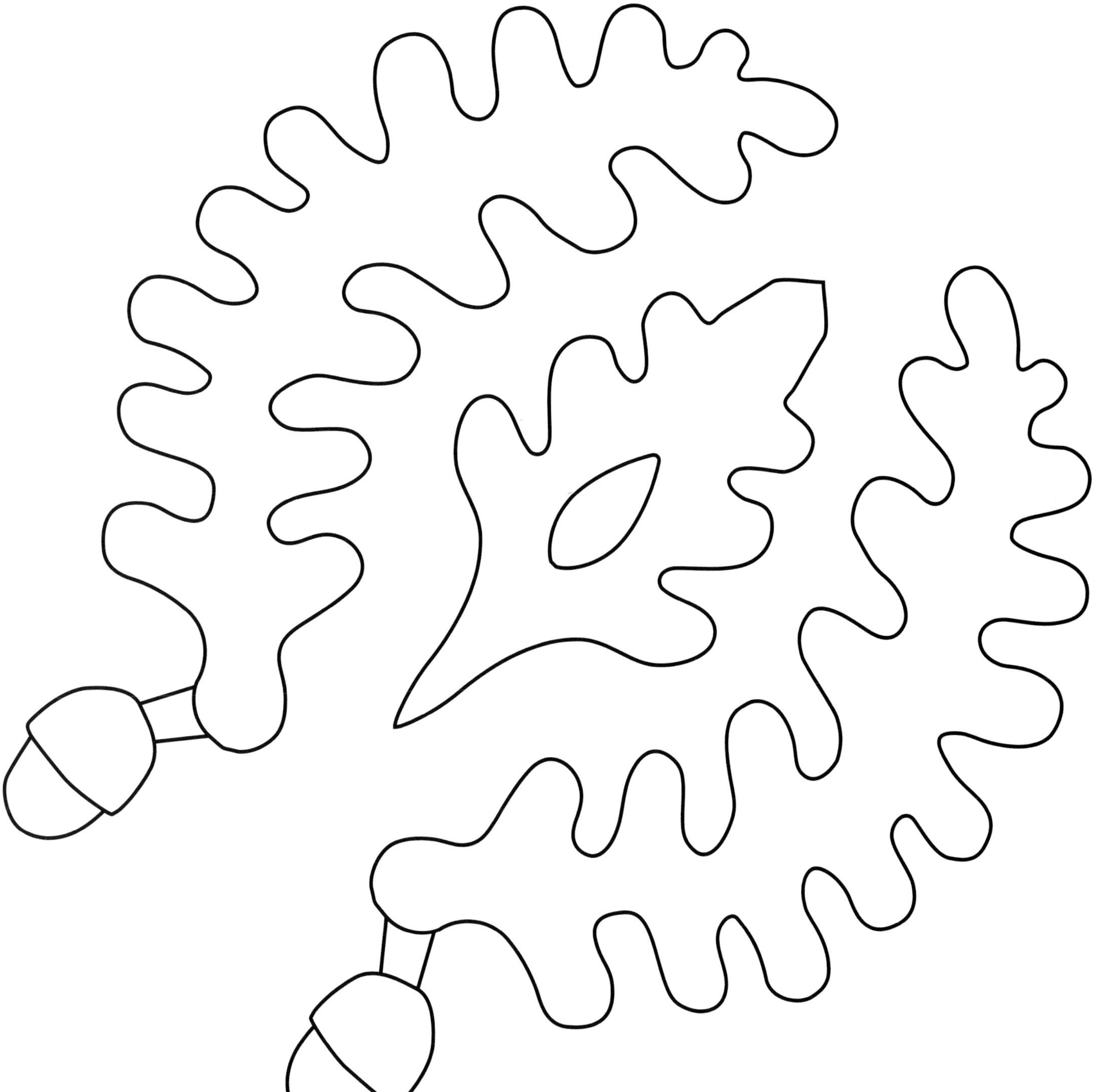

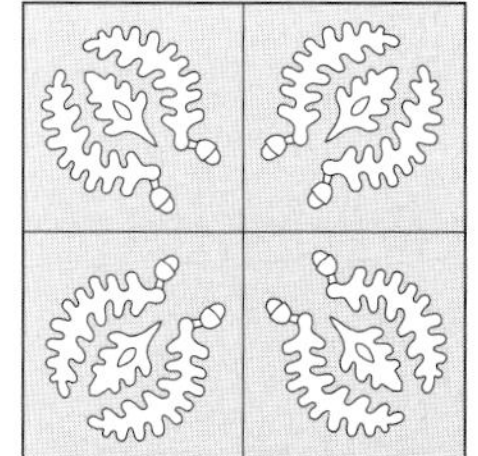

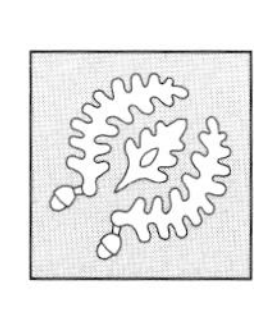

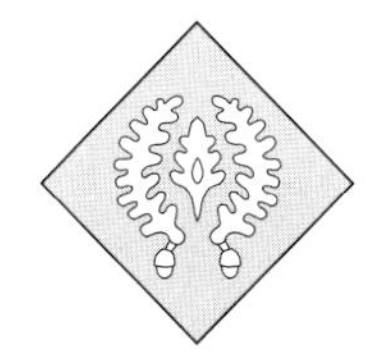

Special Note:
Reverse appliqué in center leaf.

61 

Triple Oak Leaf

Special Note:
Reverse appliqué in leaves.

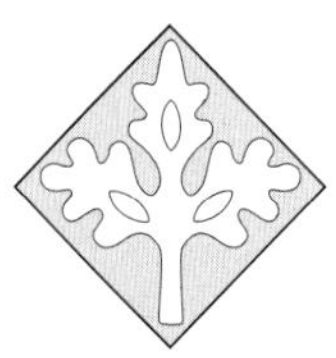

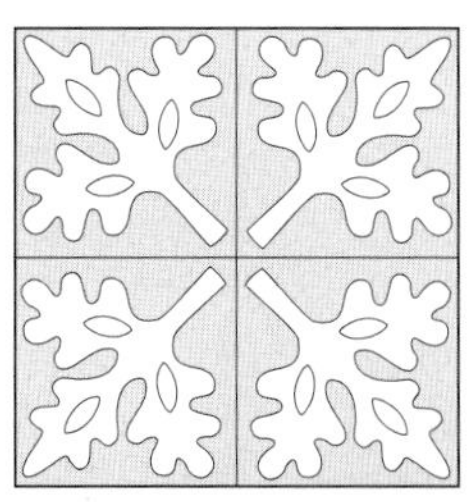

Acorn Cluster

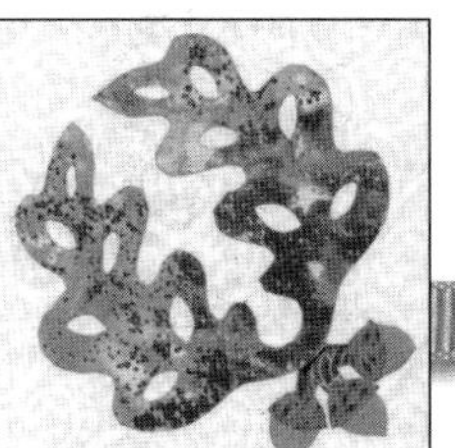

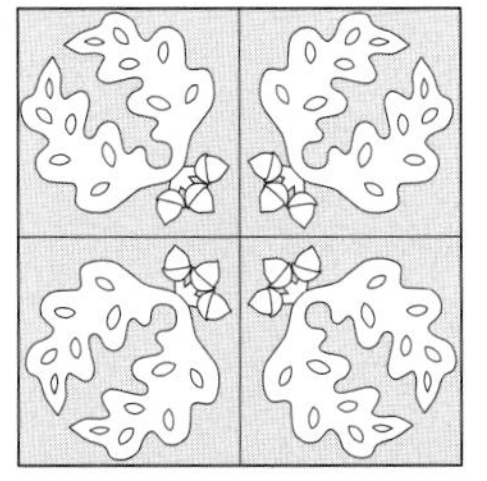

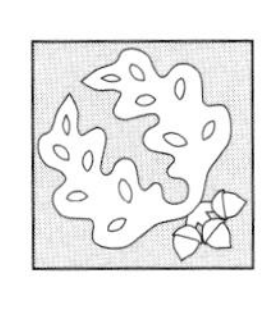

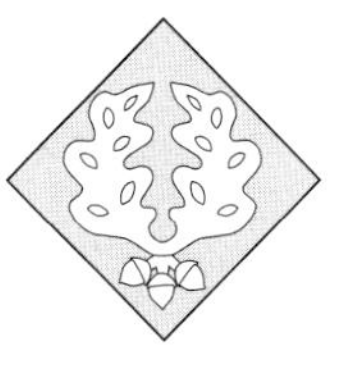

Special Note:
Reverse appliqué in leaves.

63 American Pride

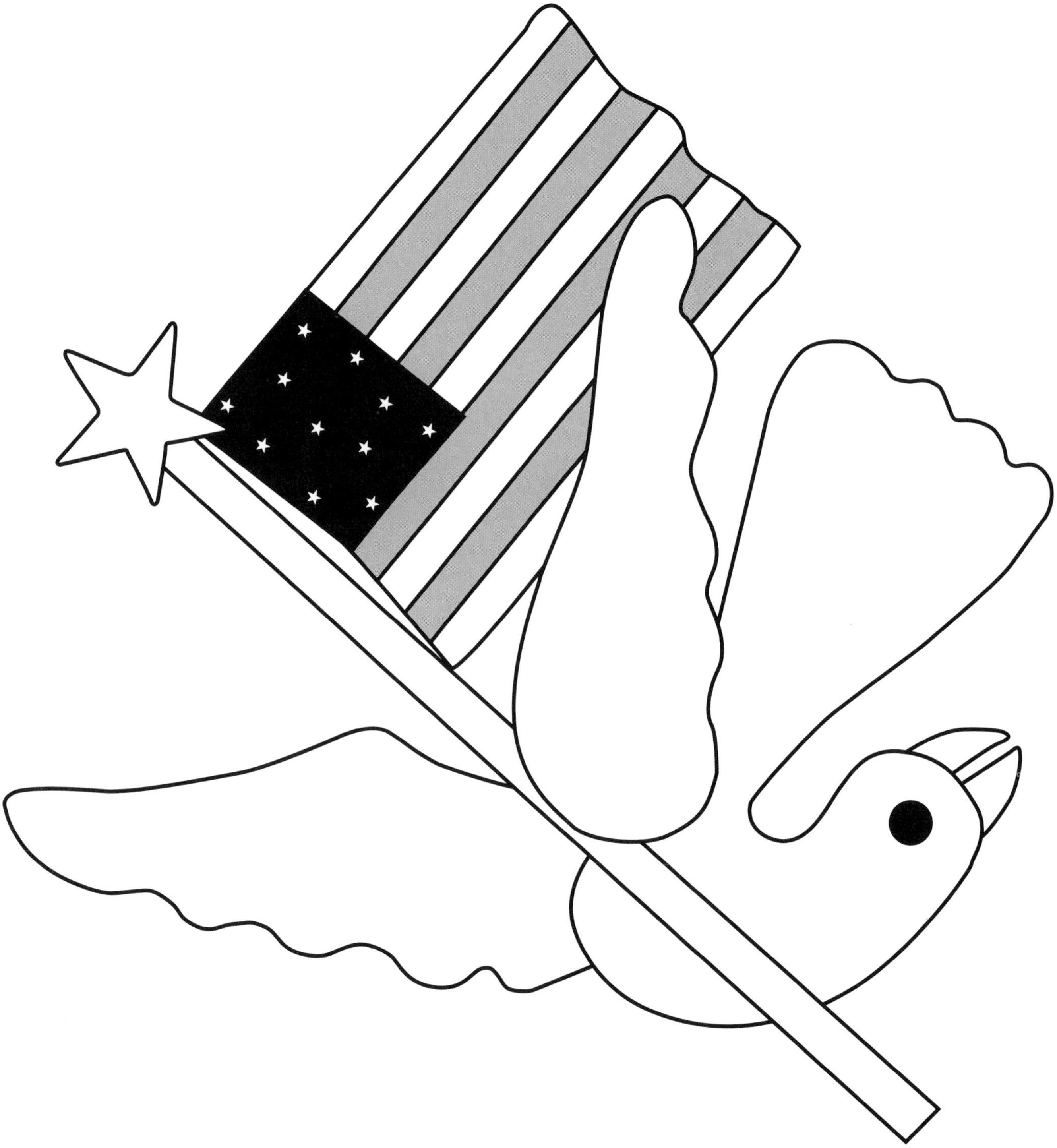

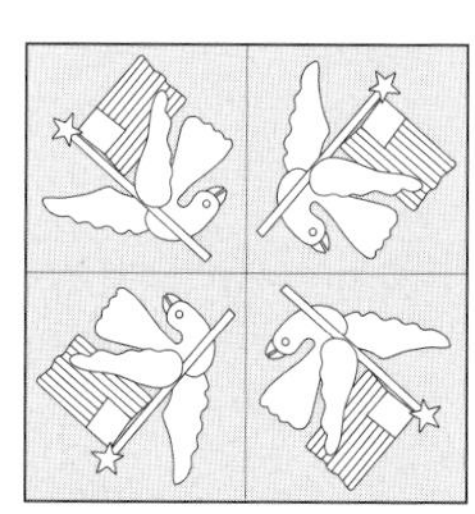

Special Note:
Stencil bird's eye, and blue and red areas on flag.

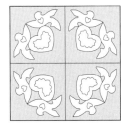

Lovebirds

Special Note:
Reverse appliqué in large heart.

65 

Trumpet Flower

Special Notes:
Use 1/4" bias bar for stems; reverse appliqué in flowers.

Country Man

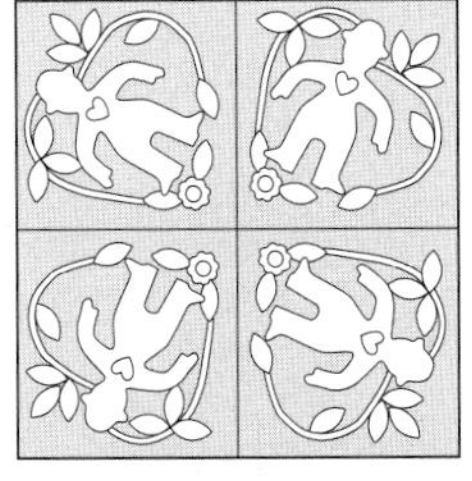

Special Notes:
Use 1/4" bias bar for stems; reverse appliqué heart.

67

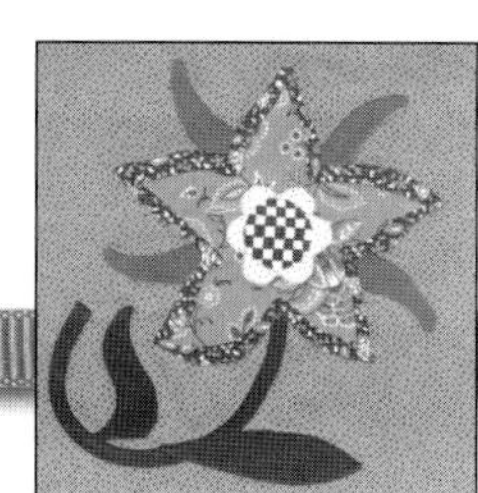

Exotic Star Flower

Special Note:
Use 1/4" bias bar for stem.

Exotic Sunflowers

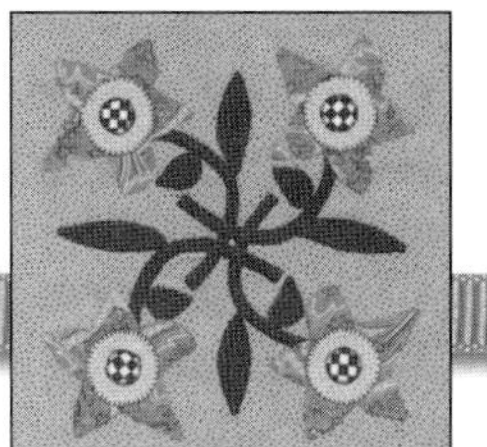

68

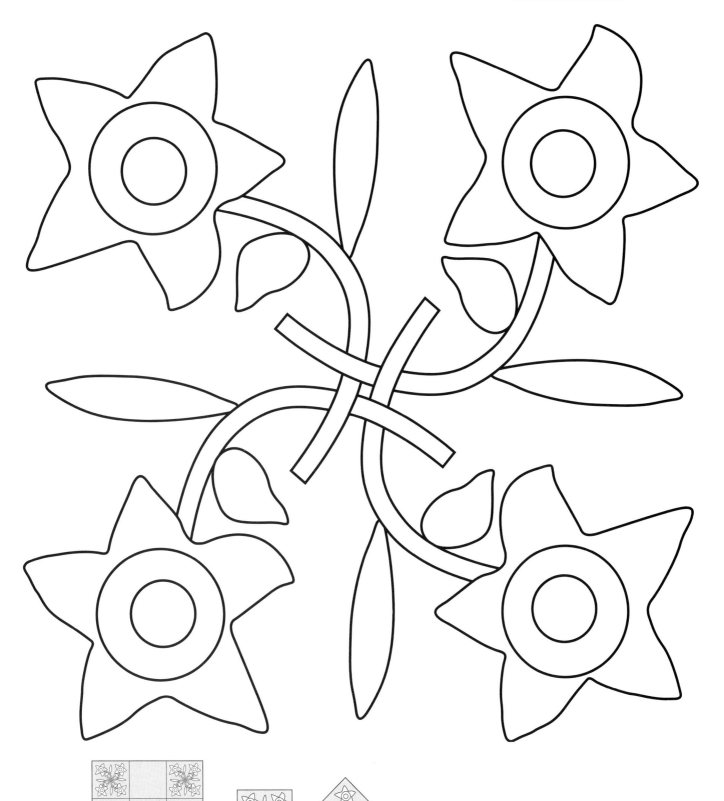

Special Note:
Use 1/4" bias bar for stems.

69

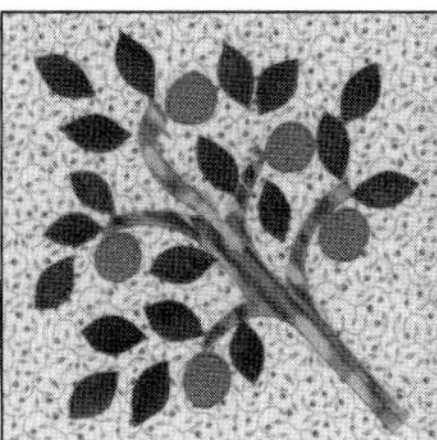

Apple Tree

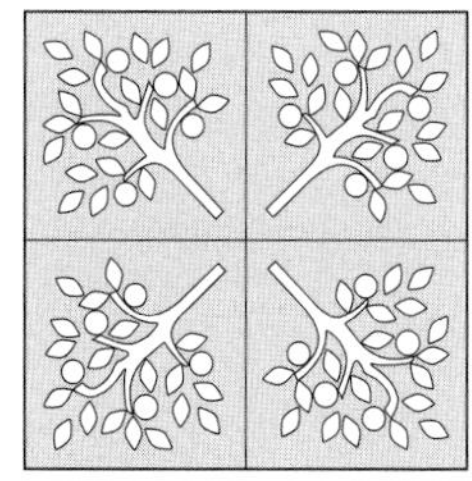

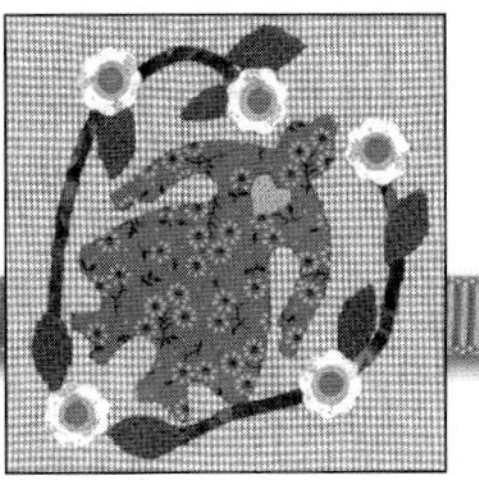

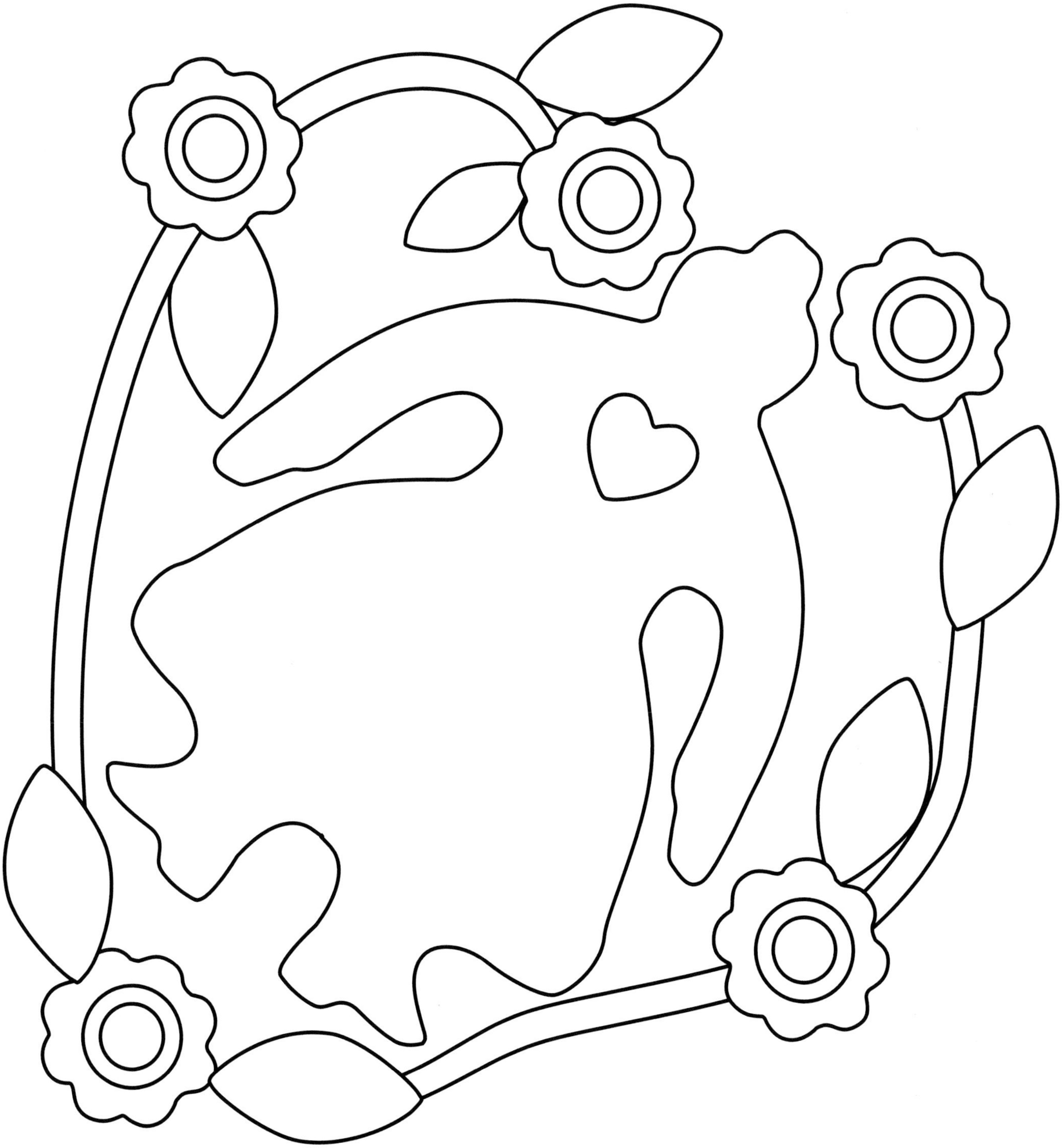

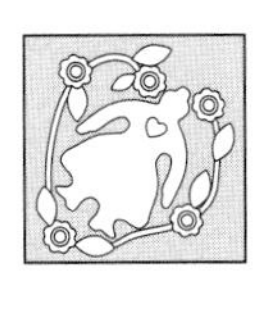

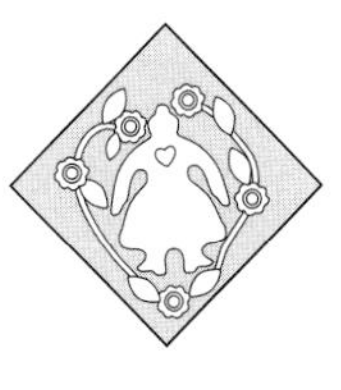

Special Notes:
Use 1/4" bias bar for stems; reverse appliqué heart.

71 

Lighthouse Vision

73

Nautical Adventure

Romantic Bouquet

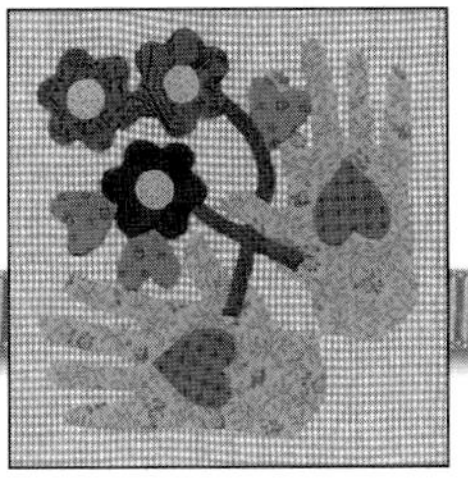

74

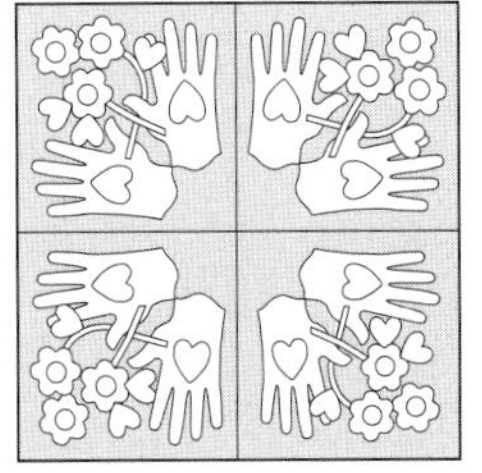

Special Notes:
Use 1/4" bias bar for stems; reverse appliqué hearts in hands.

75  Heart and Tulips

Special Note:
Use 1/4" bias bar for stems.

77  Hospitality

Special Note:
Use 3/16" bias bar for stems.

Wildflower Wreath

Special Note:
Use 3/16" bias bar for stem.

79 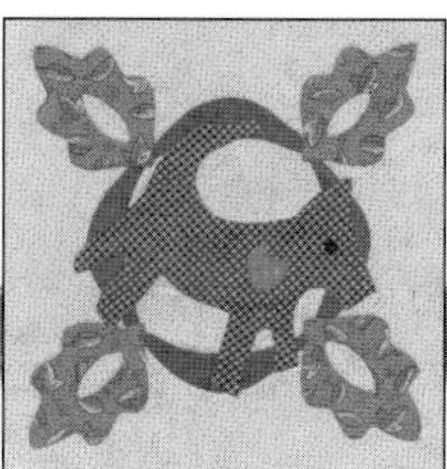 Country Pup

Special Notes:
Reverse appliqué heart and centers of leaves; stencil eye.

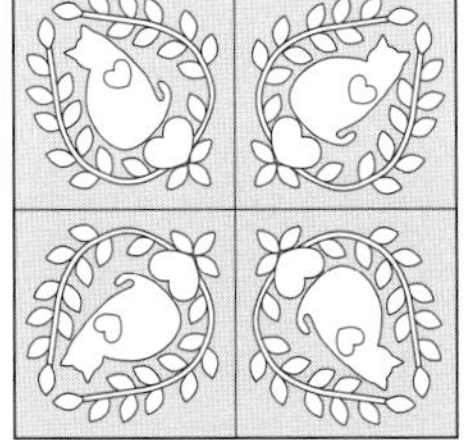

Special Note:
Use 1/4" bias bar for stems.

81

Cockscomb and Currants

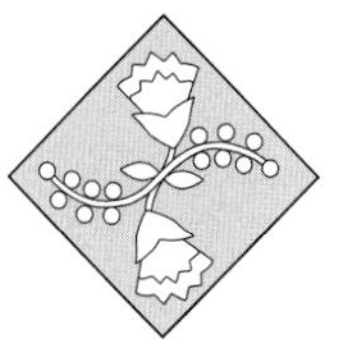

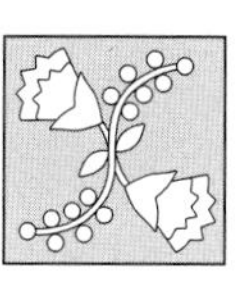

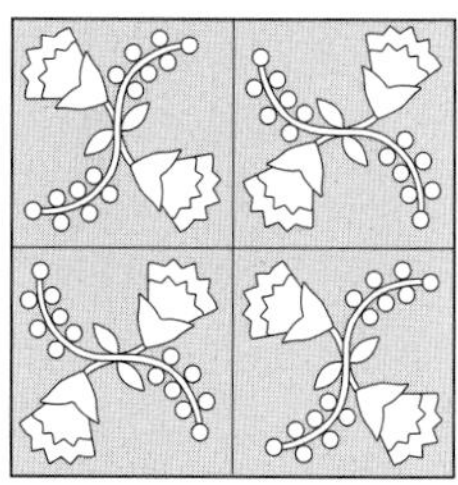

Special Note:
Use 1/4" bias bar for stems.

Cockscomb Swirl

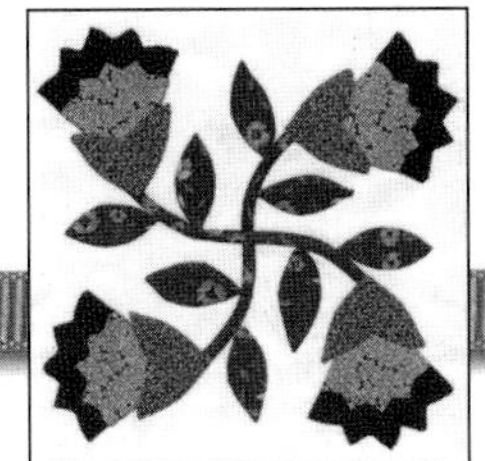

Special Note:
Use 1/4" bias bar for stems.

83 Grandma's Cherry Basket

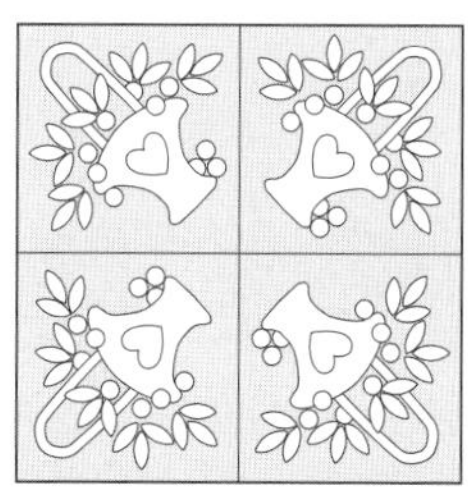

Special Note:
Reverse appliqué heart.

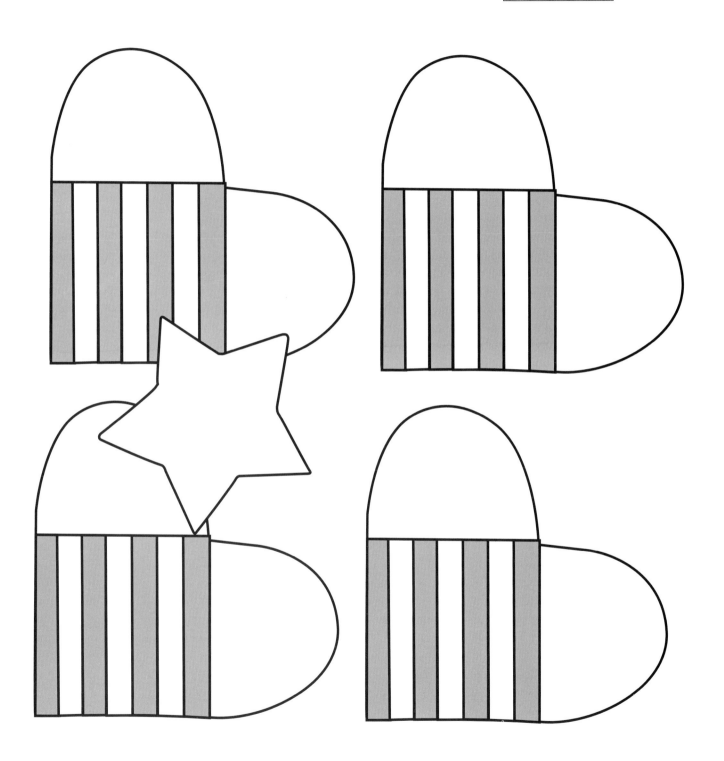

Patriotic Hearts

84

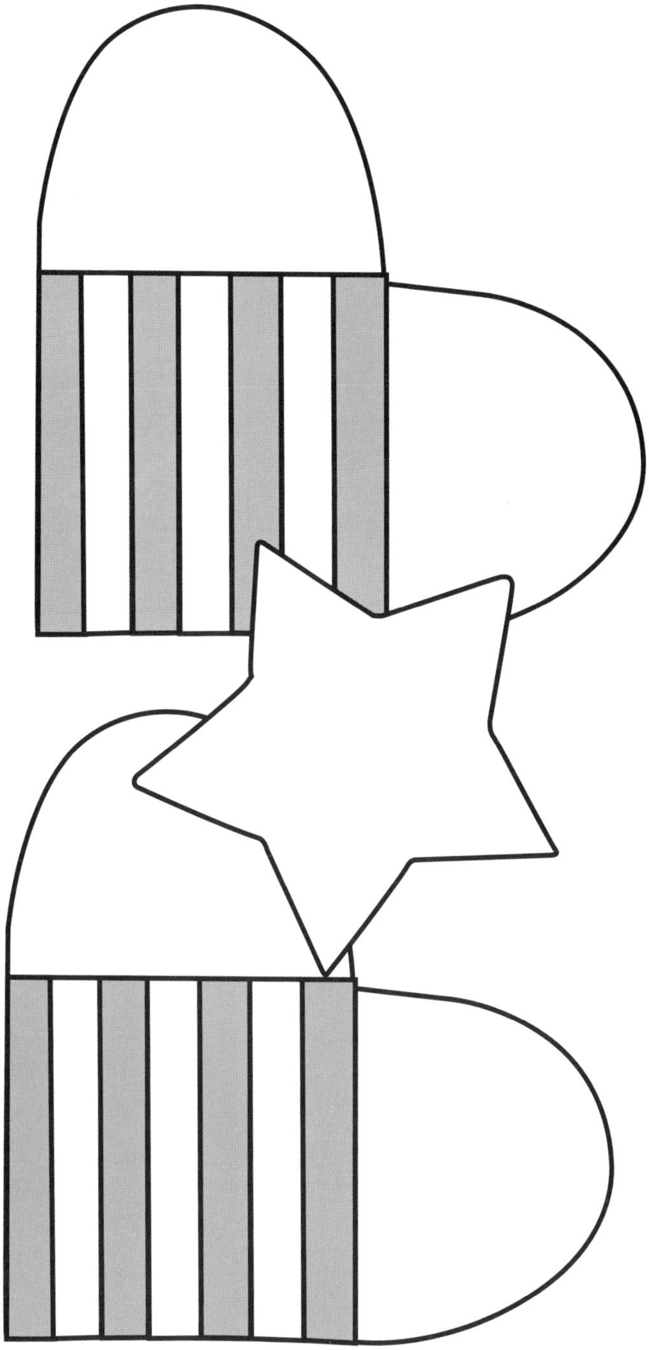

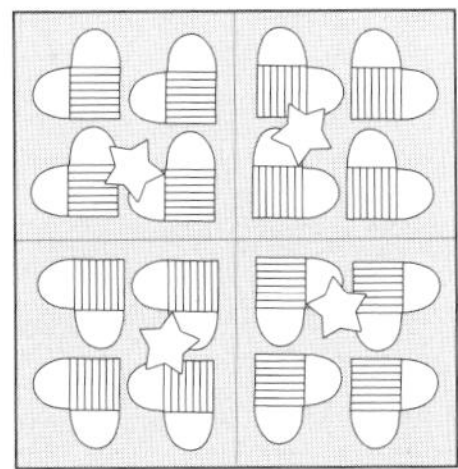

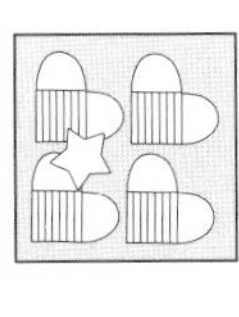

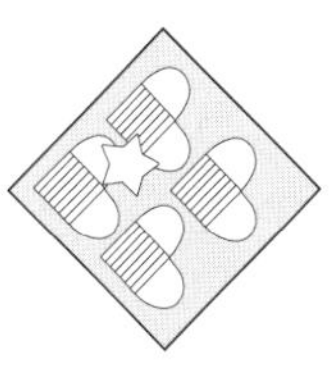

Special Notes:
Stencil stripes; use star fabric for tops of hearts.

Love in Bloom

Special Note:
Use 3/16" bias bar for stems.

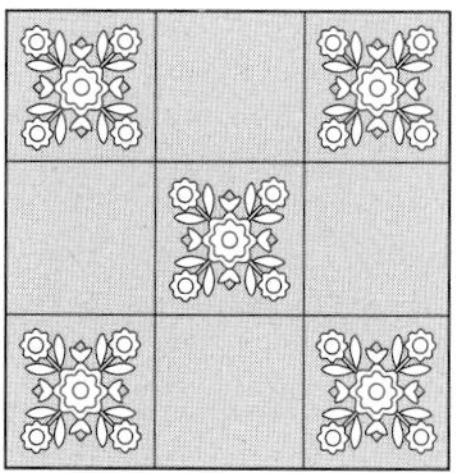

Crossed Paisley Stems

86

Special Notes:
Use 1/4" bias bar for stems; reverse appliqué in flowers.

87

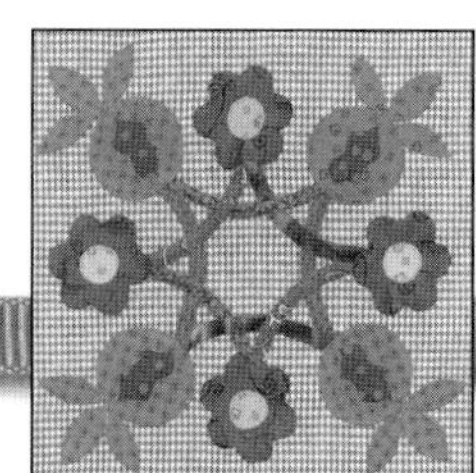

Classic Pomegranate

Special Notes:
Use 1/4" bias bar for stems; reverse appliqué in pomegranates; use four different green prints for stems.

Dancing Shoes

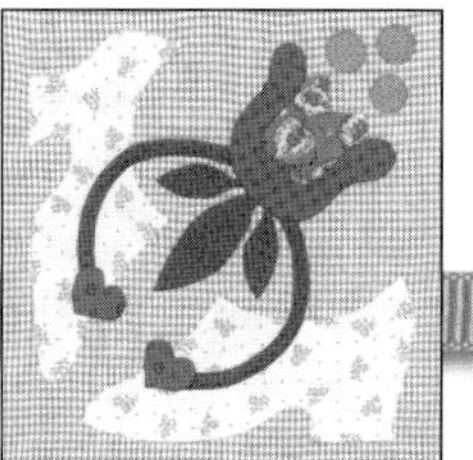

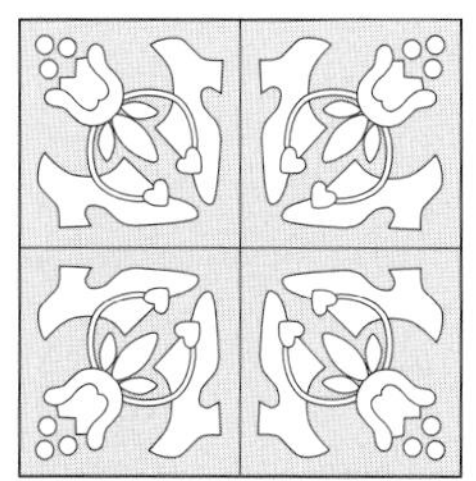

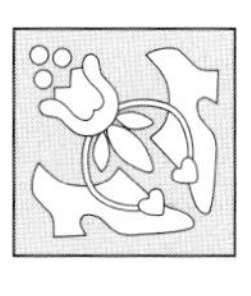

Special Note:
Use 1/4" bias bar for stems.

89 Budding Love

Special Note:
Use 3/16" bias bar for stems.

Special Notes:
Use 3/16" bias bar for stems, reverse appliqué in flowers.

91

Pomegranate Stem

Special Notes:
Use 3/16" bias bar for stems;
reverse appliqué in pomegranates.

Sunflower Delight

92

Special Note:
Stencil detail on leaves.

93

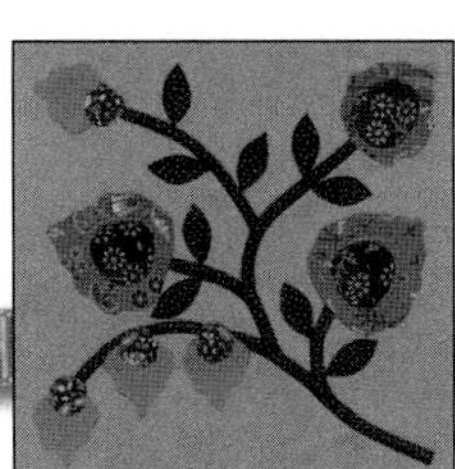

Paisley Stems

Special Notes:
Use 1/4" bias bar for stems; reverse appliqué in flowers.

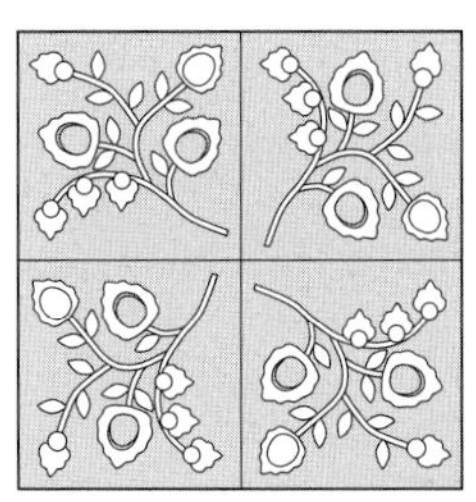

Exotic Bouquet

94

Special Notes:
Draw stamens with permanent fabric marker; use 1/4" bias bar for stems.

95

Sunflower Spray

Special Note:
Use 1/4" bias bar for stems.

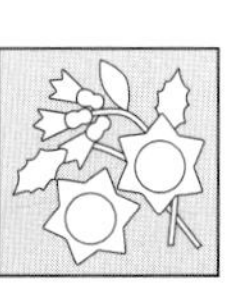

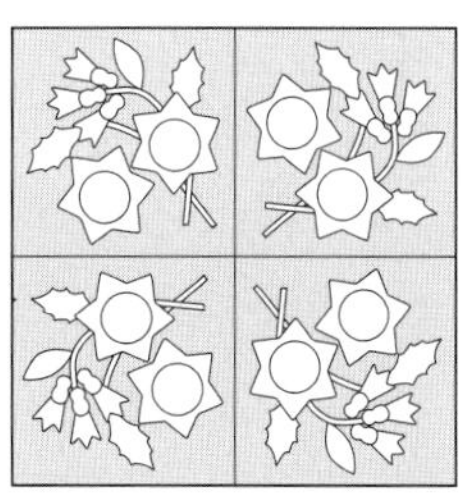

Formal Sunflowers

96

Special Notes:
Use 3/16" bias bar for stems; stencil detail on leaves.

97 Exotic Tulips

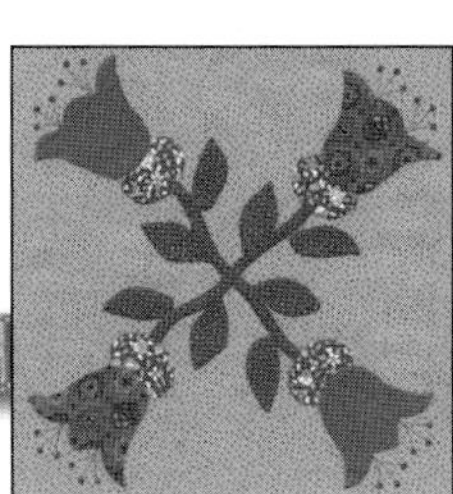

Special Notes:
Use 3/16" bias bar for stems; draw stamens with permanent fabric marker.

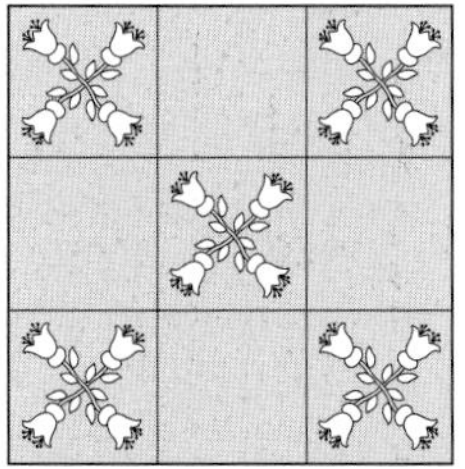

Corner Paisley Wreath

98

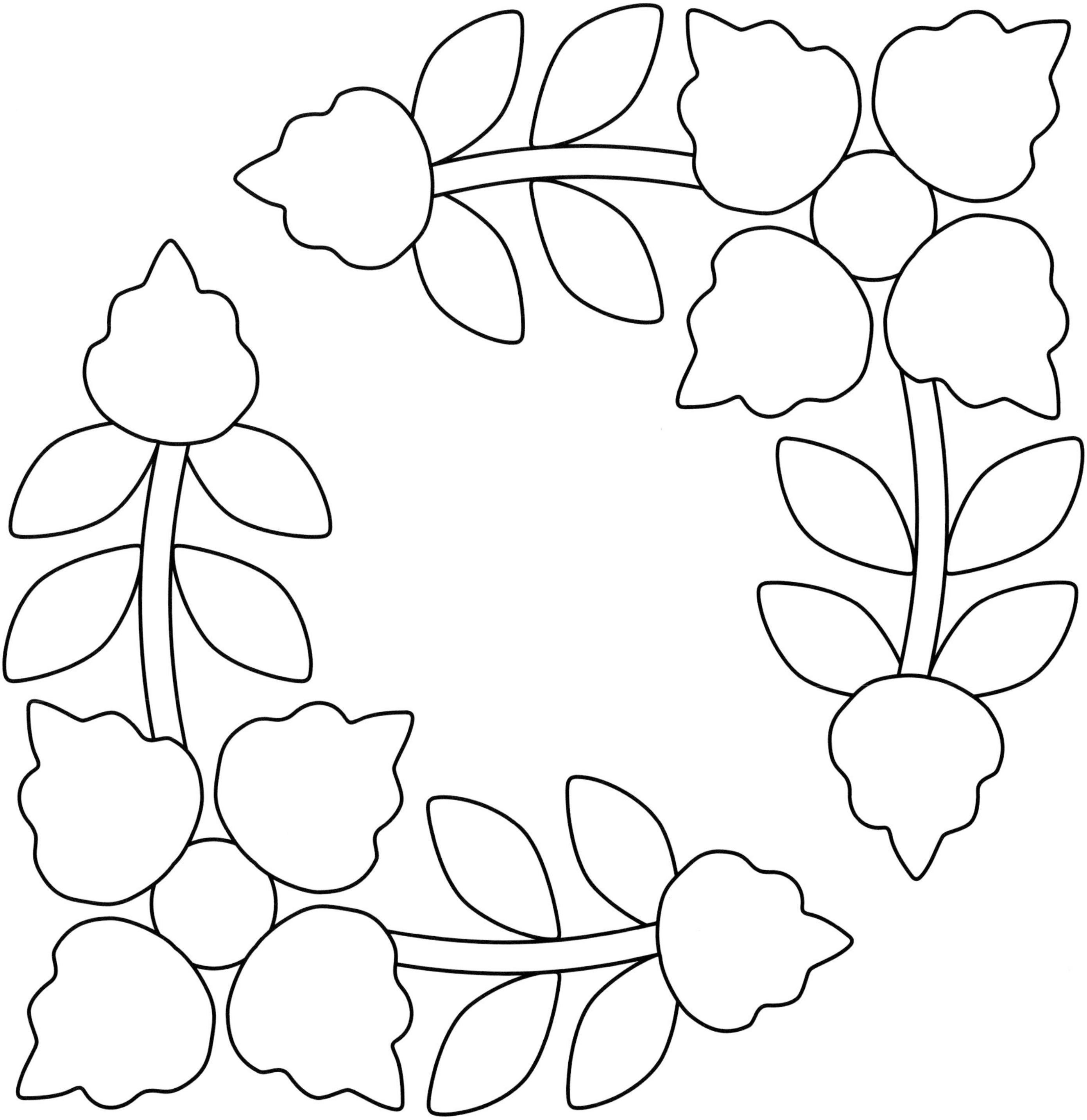

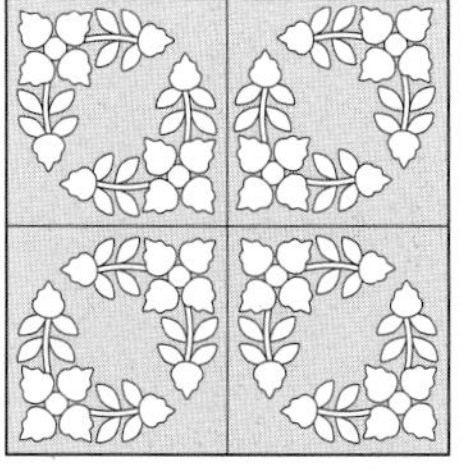

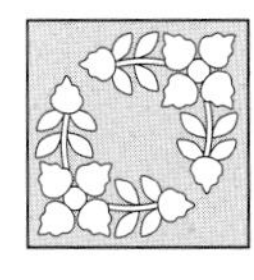

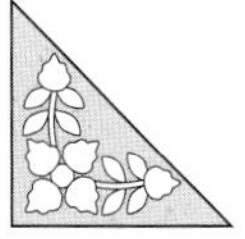

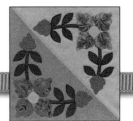

Special Notes:
Use 1/4" bias bar for stems; use half of design for triangle/corner blocks.

99

Sunflower Bouquet

Special Notes:
Use 3/16" bias bar for stems; stencil detail on leaves.

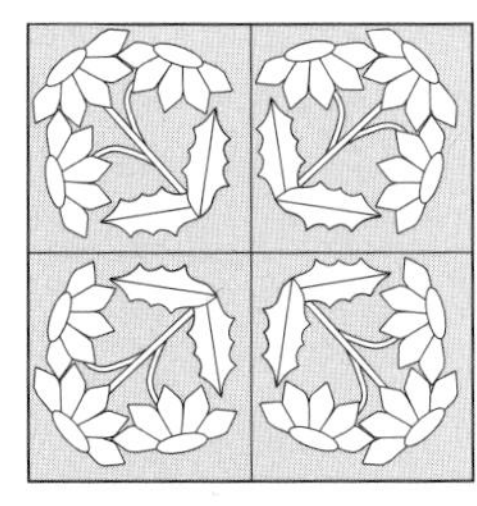

Brass Key

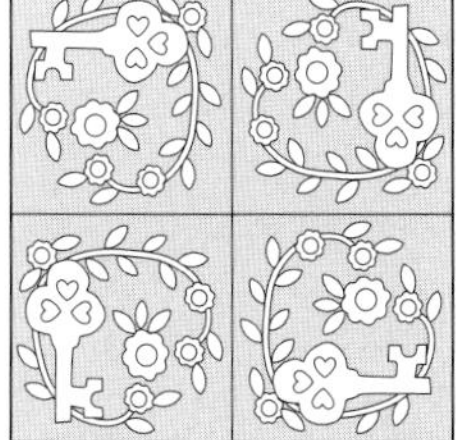

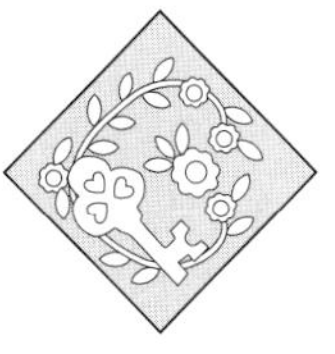

Special Notes:
Use 1/4" bias bar for stems; reverse appliqué hearts.

101 Garden Padlock

Special Notes:
Use 1/4" bias bar for stems; reverse appliqué in lock.

Finishing the Quilt

Assembling the Quilt Top

1. Arrange blocks and other quilt parts according to individual quilt layout.
2. Sew blocks and other quilt parts together in rows. Press seams in opposite directions from row to row, **Fig 1**.

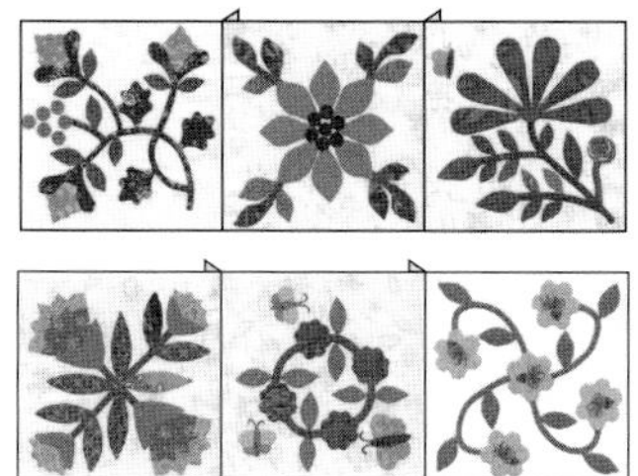

Fig 1

3. Sew rows together matching seams between blocks or added sections whenever possible.

Preparing the Quilt Top

1. Give quilt top a final pressing.
2. Prepare top for borders by making sure all corners and sides are straight and square. Measure quilt width in at least three places–across top, bottom and middle; all three measurements should match, **Fig 2**. Repeat for lengthwise measurement.

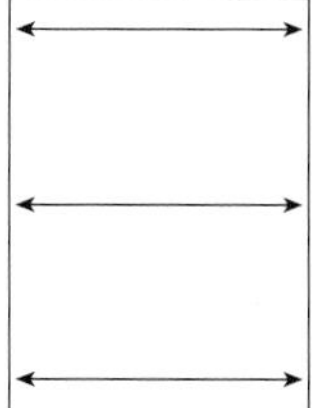

Fig 2

3. Trim with rotary tools if necessary, making sure to leave a 1/4" seam allowance beyond all piecing.

Simple Borders

1. Cut and piece (if necessary) border strips to match crosswise quilt measurement, **Fig 3**.

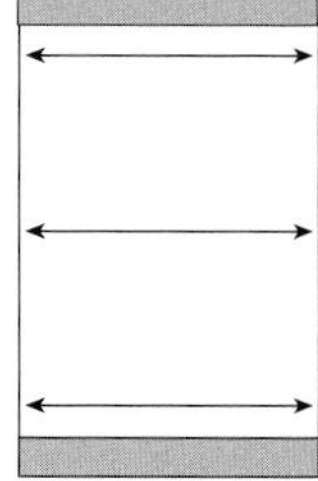

Fig 3

2. Pin borders to top and bottom edges of quilt at ends and in center.
3. Sew borders to quilt; press seams toward outside of quilt.
4. Cut and piece (if necessary) border strips to match lengthwise quilt measurement (including top and bottom borders), **Fig 4**.

Fig 4

5. Pin borders to sides of quilt at ends and in center.
6. Sew borders to quilt; press seams toward outside of quilt.

For additional simple borders, repeat steps one through six.

Borders with Corner Squares

1. Cut and piece (if necessary) border strips to match crosswise and lengthwise measurements of quilt top, **Fig 5**.

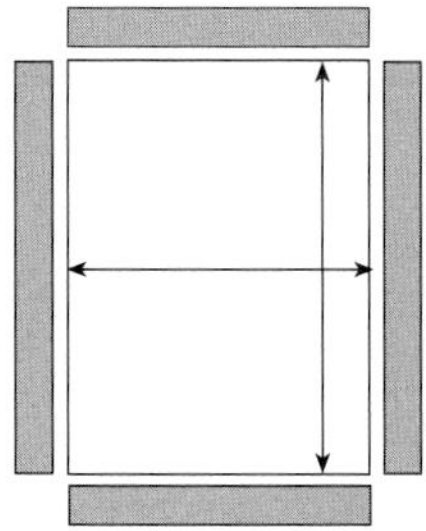

Fig 5

2. Pin a border strip to top and bottom edges of quilt at ends and in center.
3. Sew borders to quilt; press seams toward outside of quilt.
4. Cut four squares of fabric using the width of the border fabric measurement. For example, a 3 1/2"-wide border strip will need a 3 1/2" x 3 1/2" square.
5. Sew a square to each end of side border strips before sewing to the quilt. Finger press seams toward border strip.
6. Sew border strips to sides of quilt matching seams at corner blocks, **Fig 6**.

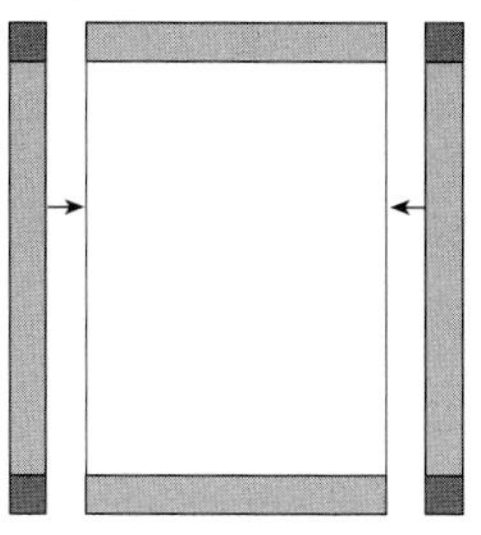

Fig 6

Marking the Quilt

Plan quilting designs and method of quilting (for hand or machine quilting) before layering the backing, batting and quilt top.

Mark quilting lines on right side of quilt top. Use a removable marking pencil, pen, or other quilt marking tool. Test all marking tools before using on your quilt following all manufacturer instructions.

Batting

Use an appropriate batting for the end use of the quilt. Read manufacturer's specifications for use. I prefer bonded polyester batting or wool batting for hand quilting. Needle punched and bonded cotton battings are good for machine quilting and some are good for hand quilting.

Layering the Quilt

Cut batting and backing up to 2" larger than the quilt top on all sides. Place backing, wrong side up, on a flat surface. Place batting on top of this, matching outer edges. It is a good idea to remove batting from its packaging a day in advance and open it out full size. This will help the batting to lie flat and "relax." Center quilt top with right side up on top of batting.

Basting the Layers

The layers of the quilt are basted either by thread or with safety pins before quilting.

For **thread basting**, baste with long stitches, starting at the center of the quilt and working toward the outside of the quilt. Create a number of long diagonal lines of stitching.

For **pin basting**, pin backing, batting and quilt tops together at six-inch intervals. Start in the middle and work toward the outside of the quilt. Avoid placing pins in prospective quilting lines. Do not trim excess backing or batting after basting.

Hand Quilting

To quilt by hand, place the basted quilt in a quilting hoop or frame. Start quilting in the center and work toward the outside edges. Using a small needle (betweens #7 to #12) and quilting thread, make small, even running-like stitches along the quilting lines. Hand quilting for pieced projects often follows 1/4" outside the seam. Hand quilting for appliqué quilts follows the appliqué edge, about 1/16" outside the design. A second line of quilting is usually placed 1/4" from the appliqué.

Machine Quilting, Feed-Dogs Up

The feed dogs control the forward and backward motion of the quilt through the sewing machine.

To quilt by machine, use a fine transparent nylon thread or 100% cotton machine thread for the top. Use cotton or cotton-covered polyester in the bobbin. Do not use nylon thread in your bobbin. An even-feed foot is a good investment if you are going to machine quilt since it feeds the top and bottom layers through the machine evenly and helps prevent puckers.

In order to fit a large quilt under the arm of the sewing machine, it will be necessary to fold the quilt so it is more manageable. If you are quilting in horizontal or vertical lines, the first row of quilting will be done in the center. Starting at the sides, roll the quilt to within 4" to 5" of center seam; then roll quilt up from the bottom to within a few inches of where you will begin sewing. If you are quilting diagonally, your first row of quilting will go from one corner to the opposite corner. Roll the quilt to within 4" to 5" of that first diagonal quilting line. Then roll quilt up from bottom corner to within a few inches of where you will be sewing.

With rolled quilt in your lap, place quilt so that you are in the correct position to begin. Make sure you have a table on the other side of the machine to catch the completed work. Otherwise, the weight of the quilt can cause a problem.

Whenever possible work from the center out, re-rolling the quilt as you work.

A short table placed to your left as you machine quilt will help support the weight of the quilt as you are quilting.

Machine Quilting, Feed-Dogs Down

This method is often called "hand-guided" machine quilting.

Place a darning foot on your sewing machine. Properly placed, the foot will not touch the machine throat plate when it is in the down position. Thread sewing machine for machine quilting. Hand guide basted quilt under darning foot, through the same steps used in "dogs-up" machine quilting. The only difference is that you control the movement of fabric along the quilting pattern. Practice.

Continuous Binding

1. Place quilt on flat surface and trim backing and batting to quilt top edge. Measure around perimeter (outside edges) of quilt. Cut, then join binding strips on the diagonal to that length. Binding width can be 2" to 2 1/2" depending on personal choice.
2. Press strip in half along length with wrong sides together.
3. Open the fold and make a long diagonal cut across the bias at one end; fold down 1/4" along cut bias edge, **Fig 7**. Re-fold binding.

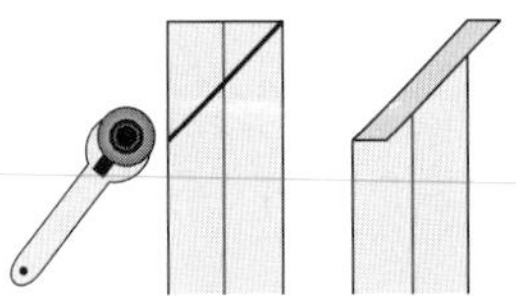

Fig 7

4. Place binding along edge of quilt back with raw edges even; begin sewing 2" or 3" from top layer of binding.
5. Sew binding to within 1/4" of corner, **Fig 8**; backstitch.

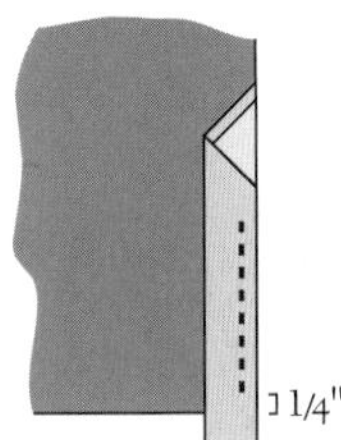

Fig 8

6. At corner, fold binding at a right angle away from the quilt top, **Fig 9**.

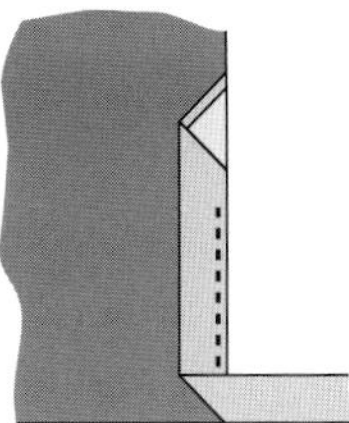

Fig 9

Fold back so binding is even with next edge to be stitched. Turn quilt and continue sewing from the outside edge, **Fig 10**.

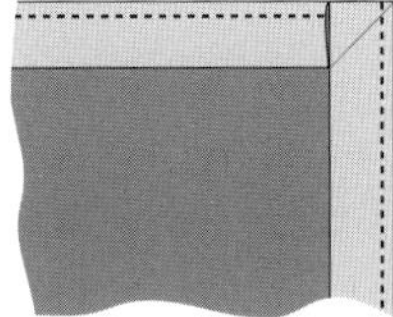

Fig 10

This right angle corner tuck will create a full mitered corner when turned to the right side and stitched down. Repeat at remaining corners.

7. To finish end of binding, tuck raw end into bias cut at beginning of binding; finish sewing, **Fig 11.**

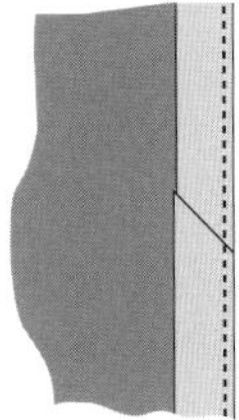

Fig 11

8. Turn binding to right side of quilt and stitch down with a hidden slip stitch by hand, or a machine hemming stitch. Close mitered corner tuck with a few additional hand stitches.

Making a Label for Your Quilt

Make a separate label for your quilt from muslin or another light fabric. Type, embroider or use a permanent fine marker for the lettering. Include the name of the quilt, the name of the quilter(s), the date and any other pertinent information on the label. Turn the edges to the wrong side and hand stitch to back of quilt at bottom right corner.